The Embroiderer's Portfolio of Flower Designs

Designs From Flower-Bed Quilt Used For Pillows

Poppy Circle, Center of Flower-Bed Quilt

Poppy Circle

(TOP) Poppy Circle Design Used On Chair Seats

(BOTTOM) Same Design, Different Scale, Equals A Hooked And Carved Rug

Marigold Quilt And Its Design Origin

Cineraria Quilt And Its Design Origin

The Flower-Bed Quilt

Eszter Haraszty

The Embroiderer's Portfolio

of

Flower Designs

LIVERIGHT PUBLISHING CORPORATION

NEW YORK   LONDON

BOOK DESIGN BY EARL TIDWELL

Liveright Publishing Corporation   500 Fifth Avenue, New York, N. Y. 10110
W. W. Norton & Company, Inc.   37 Great Russell Street, London WC1B 3NU

ISBN 0-87140-643-8

1 2 3 4 5 6 7 8 9 0

For Bruce

Other books by Eszter Haraszty
(with Bruce D. Colen)

Living with Flowers
Needlepainting: A Garden of Stitches

Contents

Introduction

It would not be an exaggeration to say that this book was born and grew to its present state in my garden. I may be a designer by profession but, since moving to California twenty years ago, I am a gardener by compulsion. If a day goes by when I cannot plant and nurture flowers, or simply watch their beauty unfold, it is a wasted, frustrating day. Since such diurnal pleasures are often ruled out by bad weather—yes, even in sunny Southern California—dormant growing periods, and household chores, I decided to transplant my garden indoors, in the form of rugs and quilts (see page 1 of color pages), furniture and pillow covers, canopies and wall hangings. It has proven a very happy solution, except when our two golden retrievers and three cats decide to bring home their favorite part of the garden: *dirt*.

In my first book, *Needlepainting: A Garden of Stitches*, I described how I began embroidering and evolved a very simple, personal style of stitchery which would not try my patience—of which I have none. The needlework designs in this present volume use the same basic techniques, but they are applied to more ambitious projects. Note, I did not say more difficult. If anything, although they may take more time, the suggested undertakings in *The Embroiderer's Portfolio of Flower Designs* should be easier to execute, because all of the floral patterns have been reproduced in full color and there are precise instructions about *which* stitch and type yarn to use *where*.

However, the real work-saver is that each of the thirty-two different flower squares which form the nuclei of every needlecraft piece in the book are, in a sense, self-propagating. Since the four quarters of my different designs are symmetrical, by using a simple folding technique described in chapter I, you may turn any selected drawing into a ten-inch square pattern, ready for transfer to canvas or linen. The resulting pattern, or an isolated element thereof, can of course be enlarged or reduced, depending upon the creative wishes and needs of the needleworker. I use that last word in the broadest possible sense. The flower squares and the large poppy circle were specifically thought out so that they might be utilized by all craftsmen, no matter what medium they prefer to work in: Needlepoint, Grospoint, Hooking, Quilting, or Needlepainting.

But this is not a book for beginners. I have assumed that the vast majority of those reading these words are already proficient in one or more of the needlecrafts and are primarily interested in special projects and challenges which go beyond the store-bought kit stage. To have included how-to instructions for all styles of stitchery would have called for an encyclopedia-size volume. A waste of paper, your time and mine, since there are excellent primers on each of the needle arts available in bookstores and craft shops. Moreover, I am hardly the expert capable of giving such information.

Finally, while I will be giving all the necessary graphic elements and instructions for copying and executing each of the thirty-two flower squares, I hope that readers will create their own designs. Everyone has a favorite flower in the garden or window box which, through embroidery, can be saved up for a rainy day, so to speak. All one has to do is make a drawing of the blossom, then trace it into one quarter-section of a square and follow through with the folding process. Now, I would be willing to wager that eight out of ten people reading this suggestion are mumbling, "Easier said than done. I can't draw." It's a safe bet because that is how my students initially respond at UCLA, where for the past few years I have been teaching the course "Design from Nature." I say to them, what I am saying here:

Almost anyone can transfer an object to paper, if he or she makes the effort to see. *Looking* is noticing, *seeing* is studying. The former is a natural reflex, an automatic act of observation; the latter takes concentration and time. It involves using your eyes to discover how a thing is constructed. Study a blossom long enough and you will *understand* how its petals and center are constructed, how shadows and sunlight change form and colors, that different colors have different intensity. When you really understand, once you truly see the flower, you will find that the knowledge is transmitted to your fingers, and they in turn, as though they had a will of their own, produce a freehand sketch. More study, and you perfect the drawing. This does not mean your rendering will be perfect, but, then, nothing is in life or nature. That is the challenge which makes people creative. What I have said about learning to see is not simply theory. By the end of my UCLA lecture series, those eight out of ten doubting students were all drawing their own designs.

Is it worth the effort? I think so and so will you, once you experience the tremendous satisfaction and pride in having turned a small square of naked cloth into a 9-foot by 11-foot rug or king-size quilt—heirlooms that will be enjoyed for generations to come. Enough talk. There is a French proverb: *On ne peut faire qu'en faisant.* One can only do by doing.

Good luck.

Eszter Haraszty

Malibu, California
1981

Acknowledgments

Primarily a designer, I feel competent and at home with needlepainting, but when it comes to other areas of the needlecrafts I need help as well as the next person. For example, I am indebted to members of the Embroiderers Guild of Southern California for the work they did on the grospoint rug and to Sandy Fox for her expertise in putting together my various quilt designs.

The
Embroiderer's
Portfolio
of
Flower
Designs

Chapter 1

Pencil to Paper to Pattern

Whether you have decided to use the flower designs provided in chapter III or your own renderings, they must be transferred first to the fabric with which you will work. To do so, use the following Folding Technique:

1. With a pencil or a fine-tipped pen, draw a 10-inch by 10-inch square on sturdy tracing paper.

2. Divide the square into four equal parts by drawing a horizontal and a vertical line through the center.

3. Now, bisect the smaller squares by putting in a dotted line connecting the opposite corners of the larger square. This last line will be used as a guide in placing the design.

4. Trace the selected design into the upper left, 5-inch by 5-inch square.

5. Fold the tracing paper exactly on the vertical center line, turning the left-hand half *under* the right-hand half. Trace the design into the upper right-hand square.

6. Fold exactly along the horizontal line, tuck under, and copy the upper two quarters into the lower two squares. The 10-inch square will now contain the whole design.

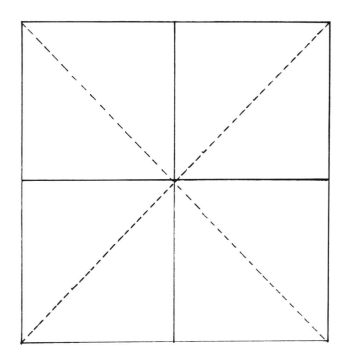

Guide for Folding Technique

COLORING IN

Using the large photograph of the color flower square (see color section following page 88) as a reference, plus the yarn charts for each design in chapter III, color-in the *entire* 10-inch square. Use well-sharpened colored pencils or a Magic Marker. Marking the whole design in this fashion is very important so that once you start embroidering you will not have to interrupt the flow and momentum to puzzle over which color yarn goes where.

TRANSFER TO FABRIC

1. After prewashing a length of Belgian linen, iron it mirror-flat. This is the fabric used for the Flower-Bed Quilt and all other Needlepainting projects.

2. Cut a 15-inch by 15-inch square from the linen. The best way to be sure that the finished edge of your fabric is straight is to pull out two threads, fifteen inches apart, and scissor along those lines. Accurate, uniform dimensions will be most important when it comes time to put the quilt squares together.

3. Center the 10-inch by 10-inch color tracing of the design in the middle of the 15-inch by 15-inch piece of linen, placing a dressmaker sheet of carbon paper between the two.

4. Using a sharp, #2 pencil or a Pilot marker pen, go over each line of the design, pressing firmly enough to leave a clear carbon mark on the fabric. Do not try to use hot-iron transfers. Some of the designs are too intricate for that process, and you need sharp, clean lines on the linen.

5. It is wisest to start by carbon copying only one 5-inch by 5-inch section of the pattern. That way you get a preview of what the all-over, symmetrical design will look like; should you wish to make changes, this is the time to do them—before more of the linen is marked up.

6. Once again, so as not to impede the rhythm and speed of the embroidering to come, I always color-in the linen tracing of the design with run-proof pens. The "Brush Pen" made by Leisure Crafts is good for this purpose. Do not waste time filling in each color area completely. A few strokes of the pen will do, for you only want to indicate which color yarn is needed where.

7. Art supply stores are the best source for marking pens and pencils, in a wide variety of colors, and for over-size carbon paper.

Chapter 2

Needlepainting: What It Is

Now that you have a clearly marked pattern on the square of linen, it is time to get started.

WORK BASKET

Having settled down to the pleasures of embroidery, you do not want to get up repeatedly to hunt for a needle or a particular skein of yarn. Keep all your tools and materials in a basket—easier than searching through a bag—close by your side. In mine I have

1. for double-checking, the colored-in, tracing paper copy of the design I am working on.

2. a marker pen, should I choose to change a line or make a note for future reference.

3. a small, sharp-pointed scissors.

4. a thimble.

5. an envelope of #18 to #22 chenille needles— the lower the number, the bigger the needle. Which you use will depend upon the thickness of the yarn.

6. a small box or tin to collect the divided strands of yarn which will accumulate as the project progresses.

7. the different color yarns needed to complete a given design. The instruction charts in chapter III tell you that exactly.

8. and, finally, after twenty years of embroidering, eyeglasses, and a packet of tissues to clean them.

A YARN LIBRARY

As all involved embroiderers know, there are many advantages to slowly building up a home inventory of the needlecrafter's sine qua non. First, the economic plus: by buying yarn on sale, or in quantity, there are dollars to be saved. Then, we've all known the regret of not purchasing a favorite, hard-to-find color when we saw it because we "didn't need it at the moment," only to discover that when we did, the store had sold the last skein. Also, how many times have you run out of a particular knitting wool, rayon, or mohair while you were in the middle of a needlecraft project? Needlepainting eats up yarn faster than a puppy does Pablum. Consequently, it is prudent to buy more than you think you will need for a certain pattern. If there are any leftovers, you can be sure they will be used in the next piece of embroidery.

To feed my needlepaintings, I visit all sorts of suppliers: supermarkets, drugstores, needlecraft shops, five-and-dimes, department stores, and discount chains, buying the colors and textures which strike my fancy. And I am equally impartial when deciding what types of yarn to purchase, for my kind of embroidery will eat almost anything: acrylic, afghan, Angora, baby yarn, embroidery cottons, knitting wool, linen and rayon threads, mohair, super mohair, metallic threads, twisted cotton, soft twist, hard twist, no twist. However, readers will be pleased to know that in addition to the commonly found synthetics (nylon, acrylic, etc.) I used only six other type yarns in the Flower-Bed Quilty. They are:

DMC embroidery floss: Probably the strongest and most durable cotton made. Colors never run. It comes in better than three hundred different shades and has such a lovely sheen that it can easily be mistaken for silk. Being a six-ply yarn, its great strength allows you to work with a single strand. I find it best for the chain stitches used in outlining a design.

DMC pearl cotton: A twisted thread which should not be separated. Number 3 is a sixteen-yard skein, available in forty-six colors. Number 5, the finer of the two, contains twenty-seven yards in eighty varied shades. There is an even thinner, though very strong, pearl cotton, #8, which not many use for embroidery. I do, however, and find the giant, ninety-five-yard balls very economical.

Marlitt embroidery thread: Four-ply, 100 percent rayon. It comes in a wide array of beautifully brilliant colors. Should you require a super shiny sheen, Marlitt will do a better job than silk. But as you might suspect, it is very slippery and prone to tangle. *Be sure* to start unraveling the skein by pulling the loose end which has a knot on it; otherwise you will end up with a Gordian knot of yarn. I know from sad experience.

Bella Donna embroidery thread: Another rayon with an excellent line of colors. Twenty-four yards in a skein, it is a very soft, twisted thread given to tangling in the hands of beginners.

Paternayan Persian: Long fiber, 100 percent wool, very strong yet pleasingly soft. A three-ply yarn which can be broken down to two strands, or even one, without the problem of feathering. The best of the wools, you have over 330 colors to choose from.

Novelty yarns: I use small quantities of Angora and mohair. They are very expensive yarns but, fortunately, a little goes a long way in achieving a lush, rich texture and look.

COLOR CHOICES

The trademark of my work happens to be bright, warm colors in great profusion: lots of shocking pink, pure yellows, firey reds, and vibrant blues. They are all there in the Flower-Bed Quilt, just as they are in my garden, but that does not mean you must follow suit. Color is a very personal thing and so is every piece of embroidery one produces; therefore, do not hesitate to build the quilt around *your* favorite colors.

As a matter of fact, any, and all, of these flower squares lend themselves to monochromatic treatment. I can visualize a very dramatic quilt which might use only shades of blue or red or yellow. One executed in just whites would have tremendous impact. If you desire a little more variety then select yarns from the cool (see Cineraria Quilt) or hot (see Poppy Circle in center of Flower-Bed Quilt) color families, *but do not mix both*. Like many in-laws, they rarely live harmoniously side by side. One other word of advice: when needlepainting in relatively small areas, like the flower squares, thread your needle with colors which are either brighter or paler than their counterparts in nature. By doing so, the two extremes will tend to neutralize each other, and you end up with colored blossoms that are very close to reality.

STITCHES AND STARTING

Because of its lush, three-dimensional quality, needlepainting may look like a complicated undertaking, but do not be fooled by appearances. It is actually the simplest form of embroidery, requiring the ability to execute only four elementary stitches. In *The Embroiderer's Portfolio of Flower Designs* I have trimmed that number down to three: the chain stitch, the satin stitch, and the French knot.

Chain. Use tiny, accurate ones to outline the entire design. Once that is done, the entire pattern is laid out before you and you avoid the possibility of erasing the carbon-paper marking with handling.

Satin. This is the most important stitch in the needlepainter's repertoire, the one which gives life and substance, movement and depth to the embroidery. Since the flower designs are intricate and small in scale, strands of the thicker yarns should be split in half before you thread your needle for the satin stitches. Naturally, if you have chosen to enlarge the pattern, say to a 20-inch by 20-inch square, such thinning of thread will be necessary less often. However, using slimmed-down strands does not mean you should reduce the number of stitches, for one must lavishly layer each petal and leaf with yarn upon yarn to give the flowers their rich and cushiony quality.

Chain Stitch

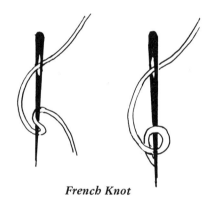

Slanted Satin Stitch

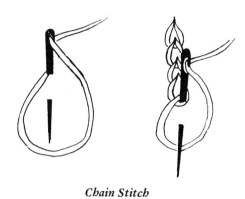

French Knot

Needlepainting is obviously not for the miserly, yet, on the other hand, it is ideal for the inexperienced. Should you make a mistake with one of your satin stitches, there is no need to pull it out and start anew, simply cover the error with a proper stitch. Also, as you might imagine, these well-padded pieces of embroidery, when used for pillows or upholstery, survive years and years of wear and tear and cleaning.

Lay-in the satin stitches, diagonally, between the chain-stitch perimeter of each petal and leaf, being careful that your needle enters and exits the linen as close as possible to the chain border. The narrower the area to be filled, the sharper the

direction of the diagonal. After each stitch, use your thumb or needle to push it aside, so that there is space to pack in the next one as snuggly against it's predecessor as you can. Do not pull the satin stitches too tightly or you will distort the shape of the linen and, of equal importance, the yarn will end up in straight lines—what you really want are curved, wavey ones to approximate the true appearance of petals and leaves. While needlepainting, I constantly over-stitch, pushing and packing the yarn, molding it into lifelike shapes.

Lastly, but really first, I usually begin embroidering from the darker centers of the flowers, and the base of the leaves, outward to their lighter-shaded periphery. There is a very practical reason for my outward progression. When one does the lighter colors and whites first, they invariably get twice as soiled as normal by the time the square is completed. Also, the very center of the flowers are usually the trickiest to do, and I happen to be one of those people who prefer getting over the worst, first.

French Knot. This is a rarely used stitch, except when I want to indicate the pollen-bearing stamens in the center of a blossom or the seed-filled pistil. It is an easy stitch to execute, but be careful to keep its size in proportion to the rest of the flower.

WHERE TO START

To dispel a sudden case of embroiderer's stage fright at the thought of the large project before you and to build up an initial confidence in your needlepainting abilities, I would begin the Flower-Bed Quilt with the least difficult of the floral squares. I call them "the five easy pieces": yellow Iceland Poppy, Iris, Petunia, black-eyed Susan, and Morning Glory. Having perfected your needlecraft skills on those, you ought to be ready for anything, including the most difficult of the flower patterns: Columbine with Poppy, Cosmos, Marigold, Tulip, Primrose, and Aster.

Should my having mentioned degrees of difficulty make you wonder if you are up to the task, please remember that there is little satisfaction to be derived from what comes easily. Besides, needlepainting is not a regimented needlecraft, where precision is the name of the game. It leaves room for error—detecting a goof is like trying to find a needle in a haystack of yarns—and room for the embroiderer to express her, or his, own creative urges. Therefore, my starting word of advice is a quotation stolen from *Needlepainting: A Garden of Stitches*: "Remember, you don't necessarily have to do exactly as I say, or do as I do, but *do*. It is the only way you will learn how good you are.

HOW TO FINISH

How many flower squares you embroider for your project will determine whether to block them after each is completed or to wait until all are finished. I did not want to crowd my storage closet with thirty-two pieces of mounting board, so I blocked them one by one. Also, before starting a new flower, it is a marvelous incentive to see how lovely the last one looks, once washed and back in shape. For no matter how clean your hands or how careful you are not to distort the shape of the linen while stitching, unless you use a frame or hoop, a finished needlepainting needs freshening up and straightening out.

WASHING AND BLOCKING

1. Fill a sink or wash pan with lukewarm water and a mild soap, such as Woolite. Stir the fabric about until every bit of linen and every strand of yarn has been saturated in suds. Overly soiled pieces should be left to soak overnight, but fifteen to twenty minutes should be enough for most. If any spots remain, rub those areas again with suds, using a firm but gentle motion. Give the embroidery a final washing in the same sudsy water.

2. Rinse the needlepainting under the cold water tap until all vestiges of soap are gone. I give mine a final rinsing in cold water with one-quarter cup of white vinegar, to brighten the colors and whiten the linen.

A NOTE OF CAUTION: While 95 percent of the colored yarns one buys today are washable, every so often you purchase a ball or skein that turns out to run. To avoid such disasters, I always test—*before using*—any yarn when there is the slightest doubt about its colorfastness. Simply run a few stitches of the yarn through an odd scrap of linen and test wash in hot water.

3. Hand-wring as much water as you can from the embroidery. Then roll it in a thick towel to soak up the remaining moisture. Leave the damp embroidery in the towel, while you prepare to block.

4. Take a sheet of Celotex—to be found at all hardware stores, and for a small extra charge they will usually cut it to your specifications—several inches larger than the piece of embroidered linen. Cover the porous board with white cloth, old sheeting is perfect, and attach it to the back with tape or a staple gun, being careful that the cloth has been stretched smoothly and tightly over the front surface.

5. Now, on that white cloth, using a soft pencil and a ruler, draw an outline of the size of the linen, before you started to embroider. In the case of the 10-inch by 10-inch flower squares, we left a 5-inch border all around, so the penciled outline should be 15-inch by 15-inch.

6. Remove the piece of embroidery from the rolled towel and place it, flower side up, in the center of the ruled markings on the Celotex cover. Holding the needlepainting in place with one hand, use the palm of the other to push out the linen, from the center toward the four corners, flattening and stretching the fabric as much as you can.

7. Using #5 aluminum push pins, sold at stationery stores, or rust-proof thumb tacks, affix the corners of the fabric exactly on top of the pencil-marked corners. Next, lining up the sides of the fabric with the guide line, tack it down in four or five places between each corner. After this initial lining-up, you will notice that the linen has shrunk more in one direction than the other. With your fingers, push and pull the shorter length until you can tack it down, evenly, along the edge line, placing additional push pins about a half-inch apart. Be careful not to tug so hard that you pull askew the threads of the linen. They must remain parallel.

8. Place the tacked-up needlepainting somewhere to dry, in the sun or before a household heater. When it is absolutely dry, only then remove from the board and run a steam iron over—not on—it to fluff up the yarn.

In case all this digital exercise is beginning to tire you out, here is some good news: embroiderers who use a wooden hoop when needlepainting rarely find that their finished work needs stretching or straightening. I am not a glutton for punishment; it is just that I find embroidery frames cramp my style, figuratively and literally. They cut down on the freedom of motion and the tactile participation which drew me to needlepainting in the first place.

Chapter 3

The Flower-Bed Quilt's Thirty-two Squares

This chapter includes all the information you will need to make any of the thirty-two squares in the quilt. The squares are presented in the alphabetical order of the flowers. You will find a list of the yarns to use for each, a black-and-white drawing of the flower as it appears in the square, and a black-and-white chart for those wishing to execute the squares in needlepoint. Finally, following page 88, there are four-color illustrations of each needle-painted flower and a picture of the actual flowers from which the design was adapted.

Unless otherwise specified, all Persian yarns are used whole (3 strands). The little circles on the shaded diagrams indicate the placement of French knots. The smallest circles call for 1 thread and 1 twist; the largest indicate a full strand with 3 or 4 twists. Use your sense of proportion for those in between. Lastly, these tables are headed by each flower's common name, followed by the Latin equivalent, unless the flower has the same name in English and Latin.

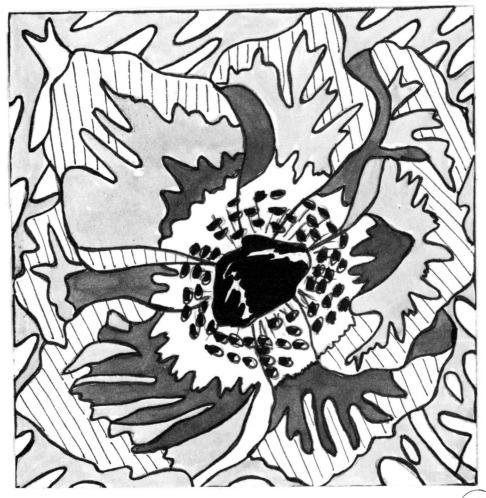

Anemone

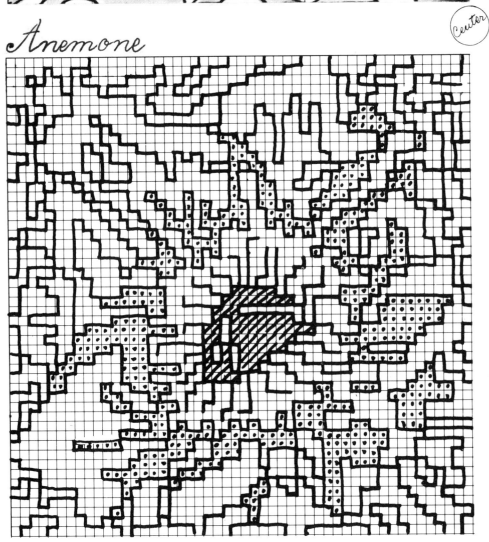

Anemone

	Color	Name	Type
1	White	Bella Donna	Rayon
2	Paprika	Marlitt	Rayon
3	Day-Glo Orange	Knitting	Acrylic
4	Orange Red	Knitting	Acrylic
5	Red	Angora	Wool
6	Deep Red	Bella Donna	Rayon
7	Light Green	Marlitt	Rayon
8	Medium Green	Marlitt	Rayon
9	Royal Blue	Marlitt	Rayon
10	Black	Bella Donna	Rayon
11	Black	Persian	Wool

STITCHES

Outline anemones with Paprika chain stitch. Fill darkest area with Deep Red satin stitch. *Lighter area* takes Red Angora doubled, in satin stitch. Hatched area of flowers requires colors 3 and 4 threaded together, satin stitch. *Center*: White is satin stitched. *Pistil*: Black, satin stitched, over and over. *Stamen*: Single thread, black, with Royal Blue French knots. *Stems*: Light Green satin stitch. *Background*: Medium Green satin stitch.

11

Callistephus „Aster "

center

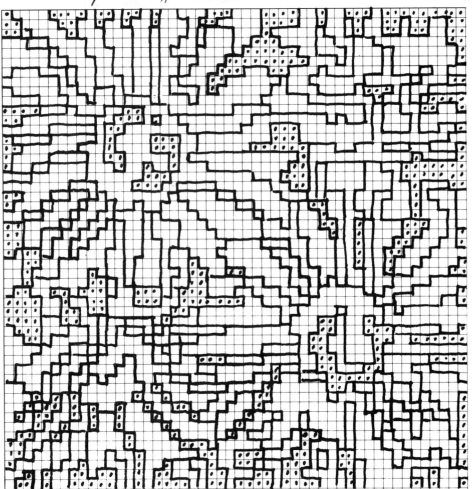

Aster

Callistephus

	COLOR	NAME	TYPE
1	Magenta	DMC Pearl #5	Cotton
2	Medium Purple	Persian	Wool
3	Dark Purple	Persian	Wool
4	Baby Pink	Marlitt	Rayon
5	Pink	DMC Floss	Cotton
6	Magenta	Persian	Wool
7	Blue	Marlitt	Rayon
8	Dark Lavender	Persian	Wool
9	Medium Lavender	Persian	Wool
10	Red	Marlitt	Rayon
11	Mexican Pink	Persian	Wool
12	Fuchia	Persian	Wool
13	Yellow	Persian	Wool
14	Light Green	Marlitt	Rayon
15	Medium Green	Marlitt	Rayon
16	Dark Green	Marlitt	Rayon

STITCHES

Flower #1: Outline with small chain stitch, using Magenta Pearl #5. Fill with Medium and Dark Purple satin stitches. Flower #2: Outline with Baby Pink small chain stitch. Fill with Pink DMC Floss and Magenta Persian chain stitches. Flower #3: Outline in Blue small chain stitches. Fill with Medium and Dark Lavender satin stitches. Flower #4: Outline with Red small chain stitches. Fill with Mexican Pink and Fuchia satin stitches. The Yellow in all flower *centers* is satin stitched over and over again, until a buttonlike cushion is formed. All *stamens* are Dark Green French knots. *Leaves* behind flowers #2 and #3 are Medium and Light Green satin stitched. *Background* is Dark Green satin stitched. NOTE: Except for Yellow in flower centers, all Persian satin stitches should be 2-strand.

13

Rudbeckia „Black-eyed Suzan"

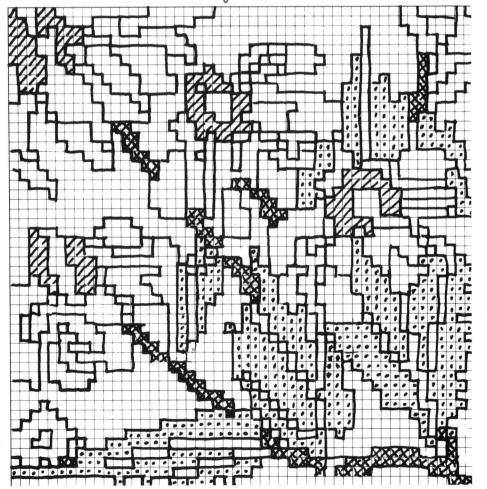

Black-eyed Susan
Rudbeckia

	Color	Name	Type
1	Yellow	DMC Pearl #8	Cotton
2	Yellow	Persian	Wool
3	Gold	Persian	Wool
4	Ochre	Persian	Wool
5	Black	Persian	Wool
6	Plum	Persian	Wool
7	Lime	Knitting	Acrylic
8	Emerald	DMC Floss	Cotton
9	Black-Green	Persian	Wool
10	Red	DMC Floss	Cotton

STITCHES

Outline flowers with Yellow Pearl chain stitch. Fill with Ochre and Gold, 2-strand satin stitches and Yellow Persian satin stitches. *Flower cones*: Black and Plum 2-strand French knots and Emerald French knots, also small Red satin stitches. *Leaves*: Outline with Emerald chain stitch and fill with Black-Green satin stitches. *Veins* and *Buds*: Lime chain stitches and, in hatched areas, satin stitches. *Stems*: Emerald slanted satin stitches.

15

Eschscholzia "California Poppy

Center

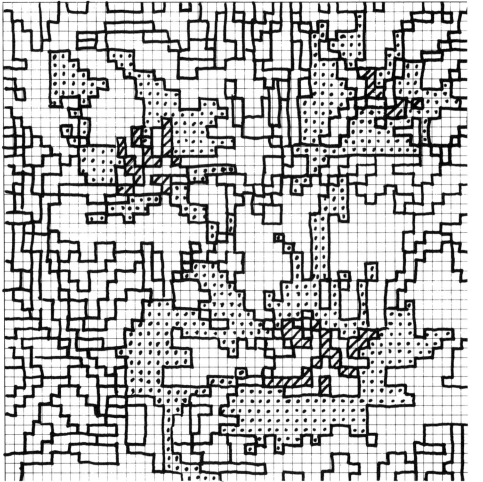

California Poppy

Eschscholzia

	COLOR	NAME	TYPE
1	Lemon	Marlitt	Rayon
2	Yellow	Marlitt	Rayon
3	Gold	Persian	Wool
4	Orange	Bella Donna	Rayon
5	Red	Marlitt	Rayon
6	Pink	DMC Floss	Cotton
7	Brown	Marlitt	Rayon
8	Olive	Bella Donna	Rayon
9	Light Green	DMC Floss	Cotton
10	Dark Green	DMC Floss	Cotton

STITCHES

Outline poppies with Lemon, small chain stitch. Fill in with Yellow, Gold, and Orange (dark and light areas) satin stitches. *Centers*: (hatched areas) Brown, Red, and Pink satin stitches. *Buds* and *Leaves*: Olive and Dark Green satin stitches. Veined leaf *background*: Light Green, 2-strand, small chain stitches.

17

Campanula medium
„*Canterbury Bells*"

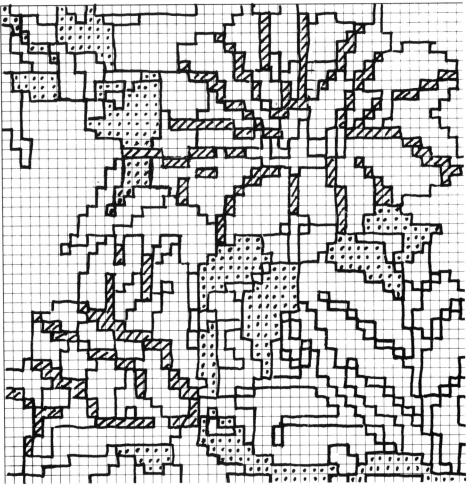

Canterbury Bells

Campanula medium

	Color	Name	Type
1	Light Lavender	Marlitt	Rayon
2	Purple	Persian	Wool
3	Dark Lavender	Persian	Wool
4	Light Purple	Persian	Wool
5	Lavender	Persian	Wool
6	Gold	Marlitt	Rayon
7	Moss Green	Persian	Wool
8	Light Green	Persian	Wool
9	Lime	Persian	Wool
10	Emerald	Mohair	Wool

STITCHES

Outline flowers with Light Lavender chain stitches. *Petal veins*: 1-strand Purple chain stitches. Fill in dark area of petals with Dark Lavender satin stitches; light gray areas with Light Purple and Lavender satin stitches. *Stigma*: Gold satin stitches. *Leaves*: Outline and veins done with 1-strand Moss Green satin stitches. Fill with Light Green satin stitches. *Underleaf*: Outline and veins done with 1-strand Light Green chain stitch. Fill with Moss Green satin stitches. *Black areas*: Emerald satin stitches. *Hatched areas*: Lime, 2-strand satin stitches.

Papaver Nudicaule "Champagne Bubble" (center)

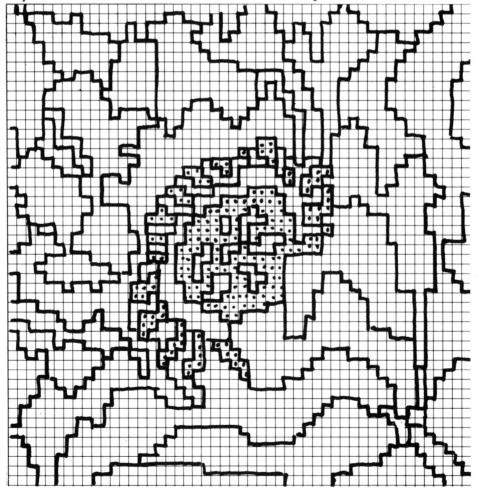

Champagne Bubble

Papaver nudicaule

	Color	Name	Type
1	White	DMC Floss	Cotton
2	Lemon	Persian	Wool
3	Gold	DMC Pearl	Cotton
4	Light Orange	Knitting	Acrylic
5	Olive	Marlitt	Rayon
6	Orange	Marlitt	Rayon
7	Day-Glo Green	Knitting	Acrylic
8	Black-Green	Persian	Wool

STITCHES

Outline flowers with 1-strand Lemon chain stitches. Fill-in with Lemon, Gold (doubled), and White (doubled) satin stitches. *Bottom of petals*: Day-Glo Green satin stitches. *Centers*: Olive and Lemon (1-strand) satin stitches; Orange French knots. *Background*: Black-Green satin stitches; Olive chain-stitched veins.

Cineraria

Center

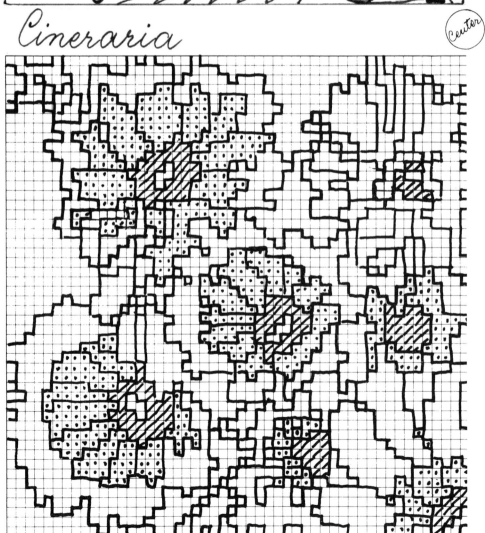

Cineraria

	COLOR	NAME	TYPE
1	White	DMC Floss	Cotton
2	White	Knitting	Acrylic
3	White	Angora	Wool
4	Pale Blue	DMC Floss	Cotton
5	Medium Blue	DMC Floss	Cotton
6	Dark Blue	DMC Floss	Cotton
7	Cornflower Blue	Knitting	Acrylic
8	Medium Blue	Angora	Wool
9	Deep Blue	Mohair	Wool
10	Purple	DMC Floss	Cotton
11	Lavender	Persian	Wool
12	Purple	Persian	Wool
13	Dark Purple	Persian	Wool
14	Lime	DMC Floss	Cotton
15	Light Green	Knitting	Acrylic
16	Grass Green	Persian	Wool
17	Emerald	Knitting	Acrylic
18	Yellow	DMC Pearl #8	Cotton
19	Mustard	Persian	Wool
20	Ochre	Persian	Wool
21	Black	DMC Floss	Cotton

STITCHES

NOTE: Reduce all Persian yarns in this design to 2-strands.

Flower #1: Outline with Purple DMC chain stitch. Fill with Lavender and White knitting yarn satin stitches. *Flower center*: Black satin stitch and Yellow (1-strand) tiny French knots.

Flower #2: Outline with Dark Blue DMC chain stitch. Fill with Cornflower Blue and Medium Blue Angora satin stitches. *Flower center*: Mustard (1-strand) and Dark Blue DMC satin stitches, with Black (1-strand) French knots.

Flower #3: Outline with Dark Blue DMC chain stitch. Fill with Purple Persian and White knitting yarn satin stitches. *Flower center*: Pale Blue DMC and Dark Blue DMC satin stitches, with Yellow (1-strand) French knots.

Flower #4: Outline with Dark Blue DMC chain stitch. Fill with Medium Blue Angora and White knitting yarn satin stitches. *Flower center*: Dark Blue and Lime satin stitches, with Lime (1-strand) French knots.

Flower #5: Outline with White DMC chain stitch. Fill with White acrylic and Dark Blue satin stitches, with Black (1-strand) French knots composing the center.

Flower #6: No outline. Fill with Medium Blue and White DMC satin stitches. *Flower center*: Black French knots.

Flower #7: Outline with Dark Blue DMC chain stitch. Fill with Deep Blue Mohair and White Angora satin stitches, with Pale Blue DMC (1-strand) French knots.

Leaves: Light Green satin stitched leaves are outlined with Grass Green chain stitch. Dark Green satin stitched leaves are outlined with Lime chain stitch.

Aquilegia „Columbine" and
Papaver rhoeas „Corn Poppy"

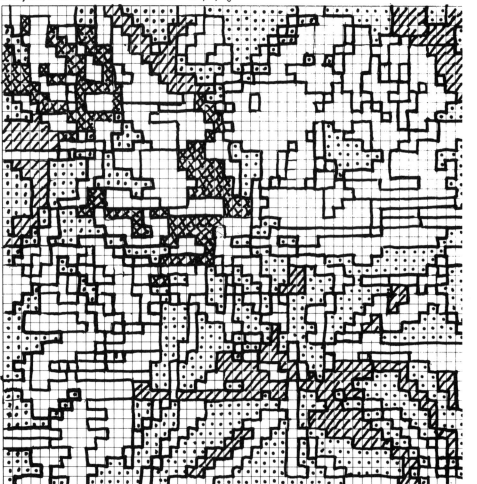

Columbine and Corn Poppy

Aquilegia and Papaver rhoeas

	Color	Name	Type
1	Dark Burgundy	Marlitt	Rayon
2	Dark Red	Marlitt	Rayon
3	Poppy Red	Persian	Wool
4	Day-Glo Red	Knitting	Acrylic
5	Yellow	Marlitt	Rayon
6	Black	Marlitt	Rayon
7	White	Knitting	Acrylic
8	White	Marlitt	Rayon
9	Light Gray	Persian	Wool
10	Emerald	Persian	Wool
11	Olive	DMC Pearl #8	Cotton
12	Lime	Persian	Wool
13	Black-Green	Persian	Wool

STITCHES

Outline poppies in Dark Burgundy using tiny chain stitch. Fill-in with Dark Red (dark gray areas), Poppy Red (medium gray areas), and Day-Glo Red (light gray areas). Use satin stitches for all. *Centers*: Yellow satin stitches with Black French knots. *Pistils*: Black and White Marlitt satin stitches.

Columbine, no chain outline. Instead, fill with White acrylic slanted satin stitches and White Marlitt slanted stitches on top of those. *Spurs*: Treat the same way, filling (light gray areas) with Light Gray satin stitches and putting White Marlitt slanted satin stitches over those. *Stigma*: Yellow satin stitches, with Black French knots. *The Greens*: In hatched areas use Emerald 1-strand satin stitches. In cross-hatched areas use Olive satin stitches. The rest of the greens (light gray areas) take Lime 1-strand satin stitches. All green stitches should be slanted.

Cosmea „Cosmos"

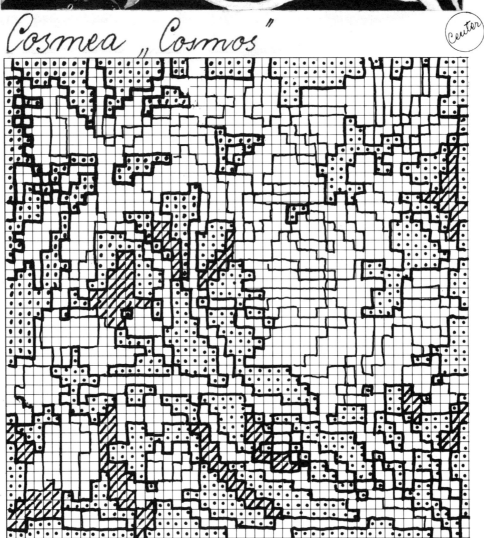

Cosmos

Cosmea

	COLOR	NAME	TYPE
1	Yellow	Marlitt	Rayon
2	Gold	Marlitt	Rayon
3	Lemon	Persian	Wool
4	Yellow	Persian	Wool
5	Orange	Marlitt	Rayon
6	Sunny Yellow	Knitting	Acrylic
7	Red	Marlitt	Rayon
8	Blood Red	Marlitt	Rayon
9	Orange Red	Knitting	Acrylic
10	Dark Red	Knitting	Acrylic
11	Brown	Marlitt	Rayon
12	Grass Green	Marlitt	Rayon
13	Olive	Marlitt	Rayon
14	Emerald	Marlitt	Rayon
15	Hunter Green	Marlitt	Rayon
16	Lime	Knitting	Acrylic
17	Black-Green	Persian	Wool

STITCHES

Outline all flowers with small chain stitch, using Marlitt in the darkest shade of each flower's predominate color. Use same color yarn to satin-stitch darker petals in same flower; use lighter shade of predominate color to satin-stitch lighter petals.

Stems, *Buds*, and *Leaves*: Use the different Green Marlitts in slanted satin stitches. *Background*: Black-Green satin stitches. *Circles* (in flower centers): 1-strand Black-Green French knots.

27

Daffodil

center

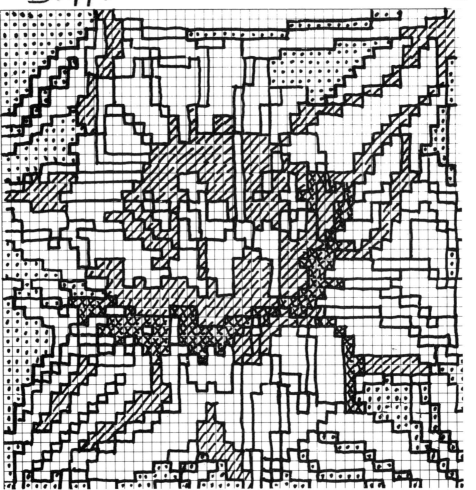

Daffodil

	Color	Name	Type
1	White	Marlitt	Rayon
2	White	Persian	Wool
3	Pale Lemon	"Souffle"	Acrylic
4	Beige	Marlitt	Rayon
5	Gray	Marlitt	Rayon
6	Yellow	Marlitt	Rayon
7	Gold	Marlitt	Rayon
8	Lemon	Persian	Wool
9	Gold	Persian	Wool
10	Beige	DMC Floss	Cotton
11	Orange	Marlitt	Rayon
12	Rust	Marlitt	Rayon
13	Light Green	Marlitt	Rayon
14	Dark Green	Marlitt	Rayon
15	Black-Green	Persian	Wool

STITCHES

Outline white daffodils with White Marlitt chain stitch. Shadows at base of center cup are done with Beige and Gray satin stitches. For cup itself, use Pale Lemon satin stitches. *Petals*: White Persian satin stitches, with ribbing (hatched area) of White and Beige Marlitt satin stitches. *French knots*: 1-strand White Persian.

Outline yellow daffodils with Gold Marlitt chain stitch. Shadows at base of center cup are done with Rust Marlitt and Beige DMC satin stitches. The cup itself is Gold Persian satin-stitched. *Petals*: Lemon and Gold Persian satin stitches, with Gold Marlitt ribbing (hatched area). *French knots*: Pale Lemon. *Leaves*: Light Green satin stitches, with Dark Green chain stitch for veins and outline. *Background*: Black-Green satin stitches.

Delphinium

center

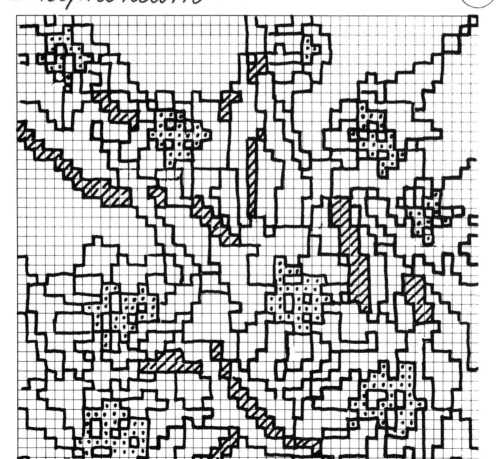

Delphinium

Color	Name	Type
1 Dark Blue	Marlitt	Rayon
2 Cornflower Blue	Knitting	Acrylic
3 Light Blue	Marlitt	Rayon
4 White	DMC Floss	Cotton
5 Black	DMC Pearl #8	Cotton
6 Light Green	DMC Pearl #8	Cotton
7 Medium Green	Persian	Wool
8 Black-Green	Persian	Wool

STITCHES

Outline flowers with Dark Blue chain stitch. Fill-in with Cornflower Blue satin stitches and in the spurs (hatched areas), satin stitch with Light Blue. *Flower centers*: Black satin stitches. *French knots*: White. *Leaves*: Outline with Light Green chain stitches, fill with Medium Green and Black-Green satin stitches.

Geranium

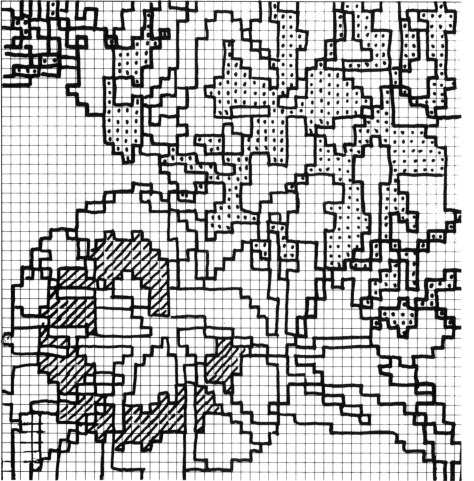

Geranium

	Color	Name	Type
1	Dark Burgundy	Persian	Wool
2	Red	Persian	Wool
3	Emerald	Persian	Wool
4	Grass Green	Persian	Wool
5	Lime	Persian	Wool
6	Rust	Persian	Wool

STITCHES

Outline "flowerettes" and some of the buds with Burgundy chain stitches. Fill-in with Red satin stitches, doubling the strand for larger flowers. *Leaves*: Outline with Emerald chain stitches. Fill with Emerald (doubled) and Grass Green satin stitches. Fill large leaves with Lime (doubled) and Rust satin stitches. *Center of "flowerettes"*: 1-strand Lime satin stitches.

Hibiscus

center

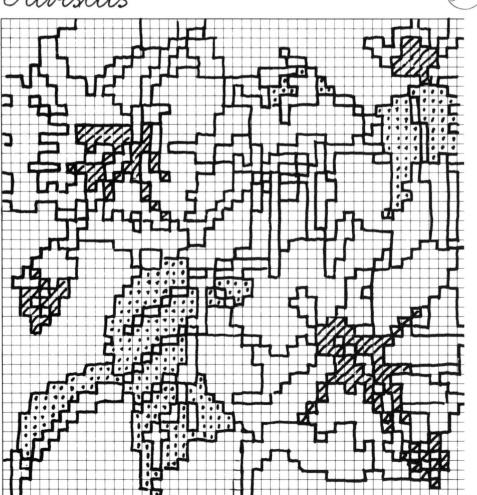

Hibiscus

	Color	Name	Type
1	Mexican Pink	DMC Pearl #8	Cotton
2	Dark Red	Persian	Wool
3	Bright Red	Knitting	Acrylic
4	Yellow	DMC Pearl #8	Cotton
5	Light Pink	DMC Pearl #8	Cotton
6	Black	DMC Pearl #8	Cotton
7	Lime	Persian	Wool
8	Black-Green	Persian	Wool
9	Brown	DMC Floss	Cotton

STITCHES

Outline flowers with Mexican Pink chain stitches. Fill with satin stitches of Dark Red (dark gray area) and Bright Red (light gray area), doubled. *Flower centers*: Black (doubled) satin stitches. *Pistil*: Light Pink slanted satin stitch. *Stigma*: Yellow and Black French knots. *Leaves* and *Buds*: Fill the light ones with Lime satin stitches (hatched areas) and for the veins use Black-Green chain stitches. Dark leaves are filled with Black-Green satin stitches (black areas) and chain-stitched Lime veins. *Cross-hatched areas*: Brown satin stitches.

Hyacinth

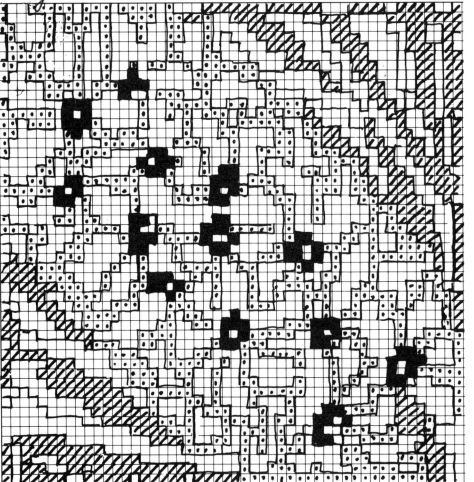

Hyacinth

	Color	Name	Type
1	Medium Blue	Marlitt	Rayon
2	Light Blue	Marlitt	Rayon
3	Dark Blue	Marlitt	Rayon
4	Yellow	Marlitt	Rayon
5	Lavender	Persian	Wool
6	Purple	Persian	Wool
7	Gold	Marlitt	Rayon
8	Emerald	Marlitt	Rayon
9	Green	Persian	Wool
10	Dark Green	Marlitt	Rayon
11	Black	DMC Floss	Cotton

STITCHES

Outline blue Hyacinth with Medium Blue, small chain stitch. Fill-in with Light Blue satin stitch, using Dark Blue satin stitches for the shadows. *Flower centers*: Yellow and Black small satin stitches. *Hatched area:* Medium Blue satin-stitched.

Outline lavender Hyacinth with a Dark Blue small chain stitch. Fill-in with Lavender 1-strand satin stitches. Use 1-strand Purple in satin stitches, for the shadows. *Flower centers*: Gold and Black small satin stitches. *Hatched area*: Dark Blue satin stitches. *Leaves*: Outline with a Green 1-strand chain stitch. Fill with Dark Green satin stitches and, for the lighter areas, with Emerald satin stitches.

37

Papaver Nudicaule „Ireland Poppy" center

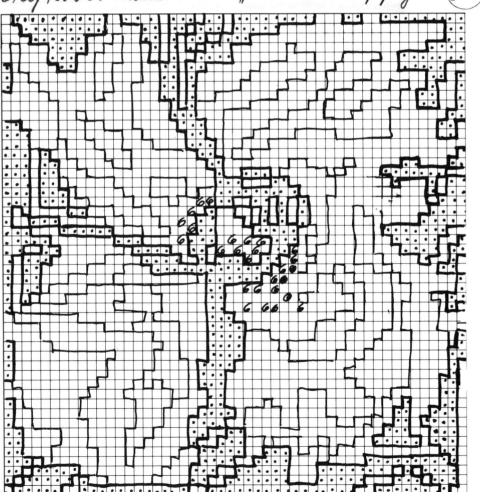

Iceland Poppy

Papaver nudicaule

	COLOR	NAME	TYPE
1	Yellow	Marlitt	Rayon
2	Pale Yellow	"Souffle"	Acrylic
3	Lemon	Persian	Wool
4	Gold	Persian	Wool
5	Orange	Persian	Wool
6	Black	Marlitt	Rayon
7	White	Marlitt	Rayon
8	Lime	Persian	Wool
9	Emerald	Mohair	Wool

STITCHES

Outline with Yellow chain stitch. Fill with Pale Yellow (doubled-strand) and Gold (doubled-strand) satin stitches. *Flower centers*: Black, White, and Orange, with Lime in hatched area—all satin stitched. *Leaves* and *Stem*: Outline with Lime (1-strand) chain stitch and fill with Emerald satin stitches.

Iris

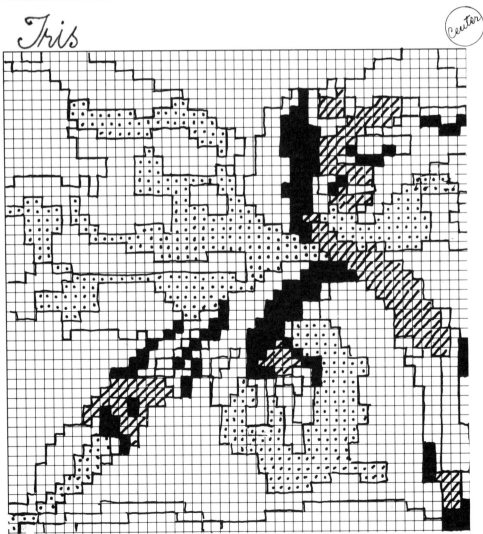

Iris

	Color	Name	Type
1	Azure	DMC Floss	Cotton
2	Deep Turquoise	Knitting	Acrylic
3	Light Turquoise	"Souffle"	Acrylic
4	Yellow	DMC Pearl #5	Cotton
5	Gold	Persian	Wool
6	Ocher	Persian	Wool
7	Green	DMC Floss	Cotton
8	Grass Green	Persian	Wool
9	Black	DMC Pearl #5	Cotton

STITCHES

Outline flowers in Azure chain stitch. Fill first with Deep Turquoise, follow with Light Turquoise (doubled)—both in satin stitches. *Sheath*: Outline with Black chain stitch, fill-in finely hatched area with Gold and Ocher (cross-hatched area) satin stitches. *Inside of petals*: Yellow satin stitch. *Hatched area*: Green. *Non-hatched*: Grass Green satin stitches within a Green chain-stitched outline.

Viola „Johnny - jump - up" (Center)

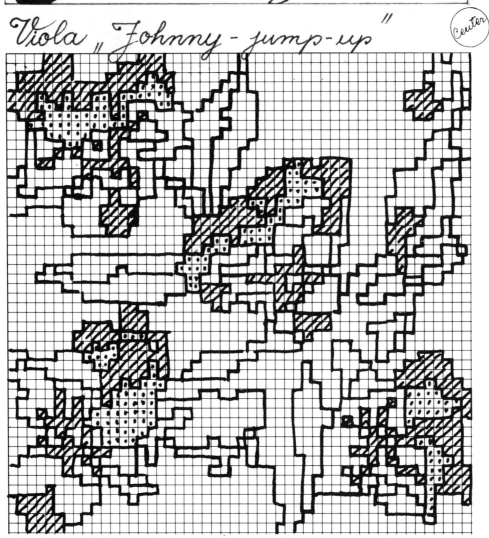

Johnny-Jump-Up
Viola

	COLOR	NAME	TYPE
1	Gold	DMC Floss	Cotton
2	Lemon	Persian	Wool
3	Gold	Persian	Wool
4	Lime	Persian	Wool
5	Green	Persian	Wool
6	Blue	Persian	Wool
7	Purple	Persian	Wool

STITCHES

Outline yellow petals *only* with Gold DMC Floss chain stitches. Fill-in with Purple, then Blue (2-strand), then Lemon, and finally Gold Persian (2-strand) in the centers—all satin stitches. *Stems*: Lime (1-strand) chain stitches. *Leaves* and *Buds*: Green and Lime satin stitches.

Tagetes erecta „Marigold"

center

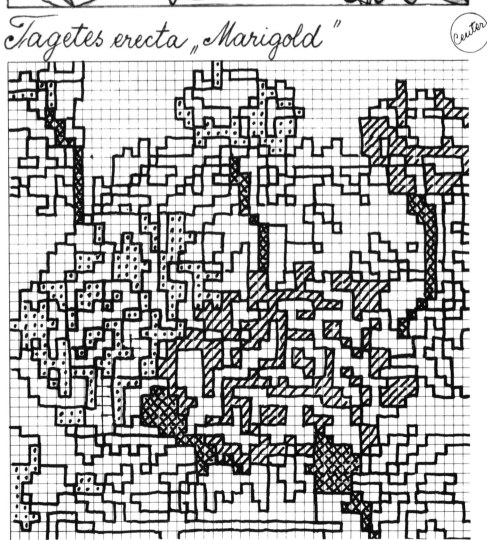

Marigold
Tagetes erecta

	COLOR	NAME	TYPE
1	Lemon Yellow	Persian	Wool
2	Light Yellow	Persian	Wool
3	Gold	Persian	Wool
4	Light Orange	Persian	Wool
5	Dark Orange	Persian	Wool
6	Lime	Persian	Wool
7	Yellow-Green	Persian	Wool
8	Hunter Green	Persian	Wool
9	Olive	Persian	Wool

STITCHES

Flower #1: Outline with Lemon Yellow (1-strand) chain stitch. Fill dark area with same color satin stitch. Fill light area with Light Yellow (2-strand) satin stitch.

Flower #2: Outline with Dark Orange (1-strand) chain stitch. Fill black areas with same color satin stitch; fill dark gray areas with Light Orange (2-strand) satin stitch.

Flower #3 (bud): Outline with Light Orange (1-strand) chain stitch. Fill dark area with same color satin stitch and for lighter area use Gold (2-strand) satin stitch.

Flower #4: Outline with Light Orange (1-strand) chain stitch. Fill dark area with same color satin stitch and lighter area with Gold (2-strand) satin stitch. *Center*: Lime and Yellow-Green (1-strand) French knots.

Flower #5: Outline with Dark Orange (1-strand) chain stitch. Fill black area with same color satin stitch; fill gray area with Gold (2-strand) satin stitch.

Flower #6 (bud): Outline with Lemon Yellow (1-strand) chain stitch. Fill dark area with same color satin stitch; light area with Light Yellow (2-strand) satin stitch.

Note: To achieve a cushiony affect in this embroidery design, all of the above flowers call for 3, or more, layers of satin stitches.

Cross-hatched areas: Hunter Green (1-strand) satin stitch. *Hatched areas*: Lime (1-strand) satin stitch. *Leaves*: Fill light gray areas with Olive (1-strand) satin stitch; fill rest of leaf with Yellow-Green (1-strand) satin stitch. *Stems*: Yellow-Green (1-strand) small chain stitch.

Tithonia „Mexican Sunflower" center

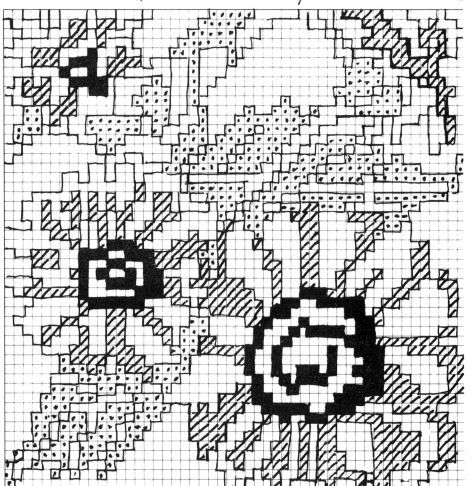

Mexican Sunflower

Tithonia

	Color	Name	Type
1	Red	Marlitt	Rayon
2	Day-Glo Red	Knitting	Acrylic
3	Poppy Red	Persian	Wool
4	Terra Cotta	Persian	Wool
5	Burgundy	Persian	Wool
6	Yellow	DMC Pearl #5	Cotton
7	Orange	Persian	Wool
8	Day-Glo Green	Knitting	Acrylic
9	Light Green	Persian	Wool
10	Medium Green	Persian	Wool
11	Moss Green	"Souffle"	Acrylic

STITCHES

Outline flowers and buds with Red, small chain stitch. Fill with Day-Glo Red and Poppy Red in slanted satin stitches. *Centers*: Burgundy, Terra Cotta, Orange, and Yellow French knots—small ones for the small flowers, large ones for the larger flower faces. In the very center of flowers, place Day-Glo Green chain stitch; fill with Moss Green satin stitches. *Stems* and *Buds*: All four greens (2-strand) satin stitches.

Ipomoea „Morning Glory"

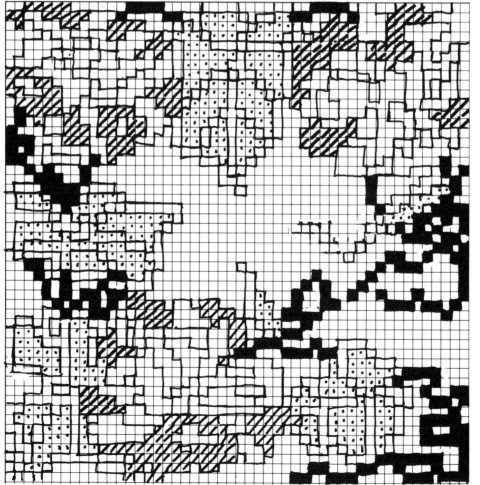

Morning Glory

Ipomoea

	Color	Name	Type
1	White	Marlitt	Rayon
2	Blue	Marlitt	Rayon
3	Dark Blue	Persian	Wool
4	Medium Blue	Knitting	Acrylic
5	Turquoise	Persian	Wool
6	Gray	Persian	Wool
7	Lime	Persian	Wool
8	Green	Persian	Wool
9	Black	Persian	Wool

STITCHES

Outline flowers in Blue chain stitch; fill with Dark Blue, Medium Blue, and Turquoise satin stitches. *Flower centers*: Blue, White, and Gray, using long and short satin stitches. *Leaves*: Outline with Green chain stitch; fill with Lime (3-strand) satin stitch. *Tendrils*: Black (1-strand) chain stitch. All satin stitches, except when noted, should be 2-strand.

49

Tropaeolum „Nasturtium"

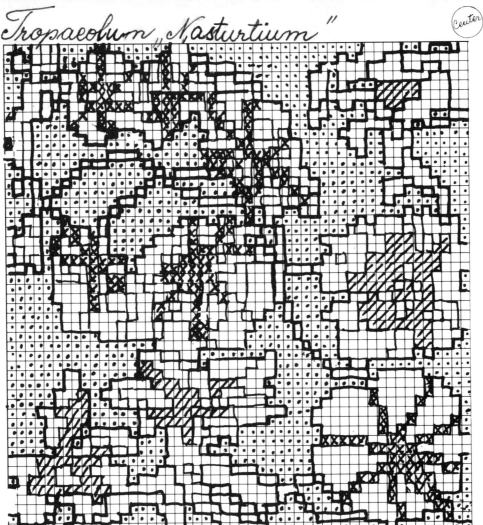

Nasturtium

Tropaeolum

	Color	Name	Type
1	Dark Red	Marlitt	Rayon
2	Poppy Red	Knitting	Acrylic
3	Orange-Red	Persian	Wool
4	Lime	Persian	Wool
5	Green	Persian	Wool
6	Dark Green	DMC Floss	Cotton
7	Light Green	DMC Floss	Cotton
8	Brown	DMC Pearl #8	Cotton
9	Yellow	Marlitt	Rayon
10	Black-Green	Persian	Wool

STITCHES

Outline flower in Dark Red with chain stitch. Fill dark gray areas of flower with Poppy Red and white areas with Orange Red satin stitches, both 2-strand. *Flower centers*: Brown satin stitches in cross-hatched area; Yellow satin stitches in hatched areas. *Spurs*: Orange-Red slanted satin stitches and Lime (1-strand) slanted satin stitches in striped area. *Leaves* and *Stems*: Outline both with Light Green chain stitch. Fill the dark areas with Dark Green satin stitches, slanted, and the light gray areas with Green (1-strand) satin stitches. Fill white leaf with Lime satin stitches. *Background*: Black-Green (2-strand) satin stitches.

51

Papaver Orientale ,, Oriental Poppy (center)

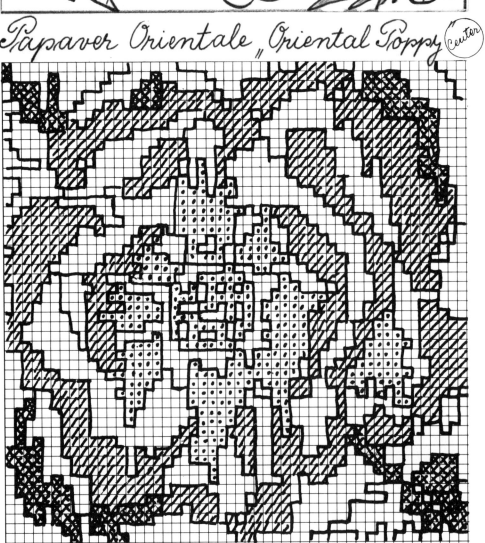

Oriental Poppy

Papaver Orientale

	Color	Name	Type
1	Light Salmon	DMC Pearl #8	Cotton
2	Baby Pink	Mohair	Wool
3	Medium Salmon	Persian	Wool
4	Dark Salmon	Persian	Wool
5	Lavender	Persian	Wool
6	Purple	Persian	Wool
7	Plum	Persian	Wool
8	Black	DMC Pearl #8	Cotton
9	Light Green	Persian	Wool
10	Olive Green	Persian	Wool

STITCHES

Outline flower with Light Salmon chain stitch. Fill with Dark Salmon, Medium Salmon, and Baby Pink (doubled) satin stitches. *Flower center*: Outline seed pod with Black chain stitch; fill with Lavender (1-strand) and Light Green (1-strand) satin stitches.

Base of petals: Fill with Purple (cross-hatched area) and Plum satin stitches. *Leaves* and *Buds*: Outline with Olive Green (1-strand) chain stitch. Fill with Olive Green and Light Green (hatched area) satin stitches.

Vinca „Periwinkle"

ceuter

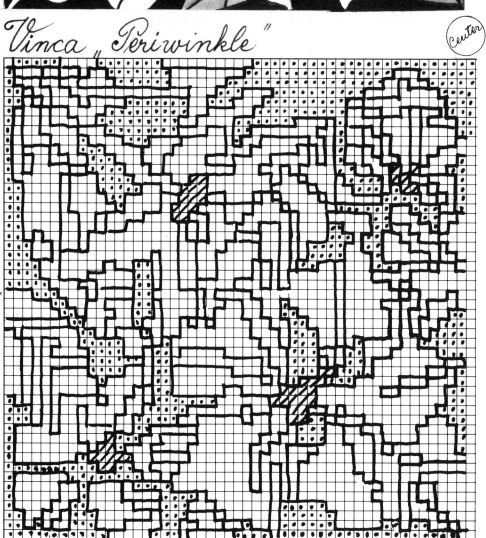

Periwinkle

Vinca

	Color	Name	Type
1	White	Bella Donna	Rayon
2	Gray	Marlitt	Rayon
3	Yellow	Persian	Wool
4	Light Green	Marlitt	Rayon
5	Emerald	Marlitt	Rayon
6	Black-Green	Persian	Wool

STITCHES

Outline flowers with Gray chain stitch. Fill with White and Gray slanted satin stitches. *Flower centers*: Yellow (1-strand) satin stitches, with Black-Green French knots. *Leaves*: Outline, and make veins, with Light Green chain stitches; fill with Emerald satin stitches. *Hatched areas*: Light Green satin stitches.

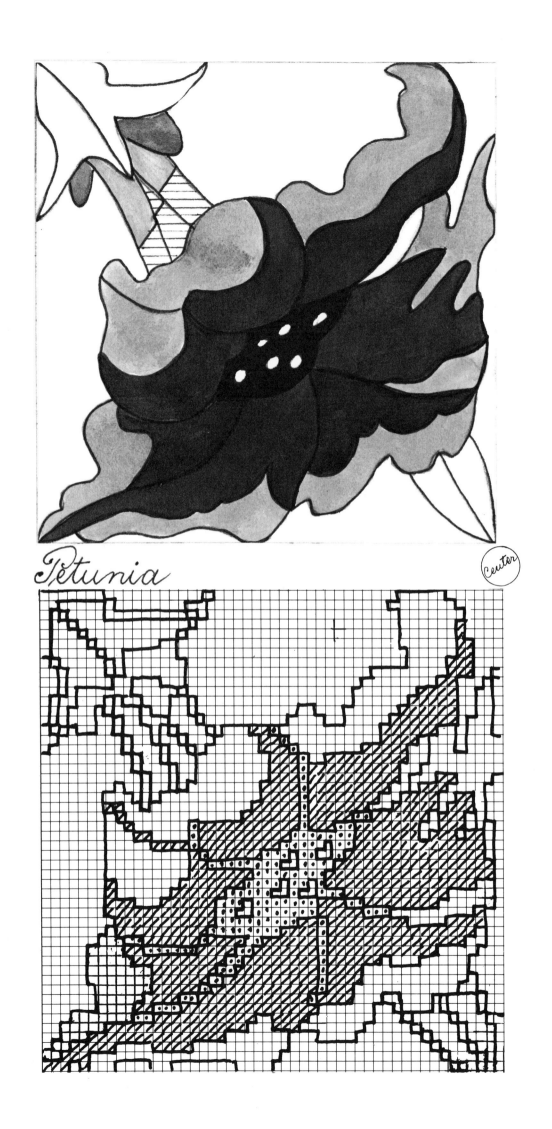

Petunia

center

Petunia

	Color	Name	Type
1	Navy Blue	Persian	Wool
2	Purple	Persian	Wool
3	Cornflower Blue	Persian	Wool
4	Royal Blue	Mohair	Wool
5	Lavender	Persian	Wool
6	Hunter Green	Persian	Wool
7	Grass Green	Persian	Wool
8	Lime	Persian	Wool

STITCHES

Outline flowers with Navy Blue (2-strand) chain stitch. Fill dark areas with Purple and Cornflower Blue (2-strands each) threaded together, satin stitches. *Cup*: Cornflower Blue in shaded area and Lavender in hatched area, using 2-strand satin stitches for both. *Leaves*: Outline with Hunter Green (2-strand) chain stitch; fill with Grass Green satin stitches. *Centers*: Fill with Navy Blue (2-strand) satin stitches and Lime (1-strand) French knots.

Primula "Primrose"

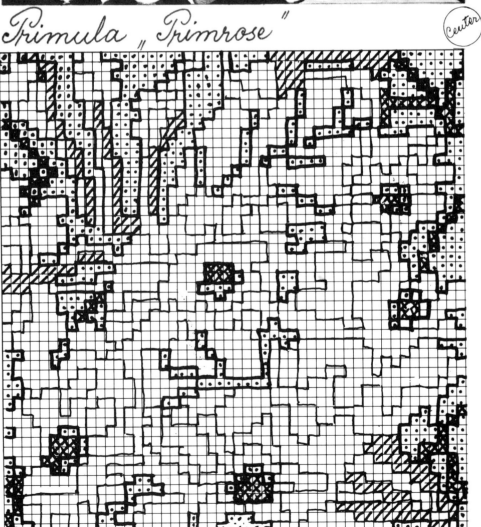

Primrose*

Primula

	Color	Name	Type
1	White	Marlitt	Rayon
2	Off-White	Persian	Wool
3	Lemon	Persian	Wool
4	Gold	Marlitt	Rayon
5	Yellow	Marlitt	Rayon
6	Yellow	Persian	Wool
7	Gold	Persian	Wool
8	Red	Persian	Wool
9	Orange	Persian	Wool
10	Paprika	Knitting	Acrylic
11	Magenta	Marlitt	Rayon
12	Light Pink	Persian	Wool
13	Medium Pink	Persian	Wool
14	Baby Pink	Marlitt	Rayon
15	Mexican Pink	Persian	Wool
16	Magenta	Persian	Wool
17	Emerald	Marlitt	Rayon
18	Lime	Persian	Wool
19	Green	Persian	Wool
20	Olive	Persian	Wool
21	Black-Green	Persian	Wool
22	Black	DMC Floss	Cotton

STITCHES

Flower #1: Outline with White chain stitch. Fill with Off-White and Lemon satin stitches. *Center*: Gold Marlitt satin stitches.

Flower #2: Outline with Yellow Marlitt chain stitch. Fill with Yellow Persian and Gold Persian satin stitches. *Center*: Gold Marlitt satin stitches.

Flower #3: Outline with Gold Marlitt chain stitch. Fill with Orange and Paprika satin stitches. *Center*: Yellow Marlitt satin stitches.

Flower #4: Outline with Magenta Marlitt chain stitch. Fill with Light Pink and Medium Pink satin stitches.

Flower #5: Outline with Gold Marlitt chain stitch. Fill with Orange and Paprika satin stitches. *Center*: Gold Marlitt satin stitches.

Flower #6: Outline with Baby Pink chain stitch. Fill with Mexican Pink and Magenta Persian satin stitches. *Center*: Gold Marlitt satin stitches.

Pistils: In all flowers use Lime (1-strand) satin stitch; and over-stitch with Black satin stitches. *Leaves* and *Buds*: Fill lighter ones with Lime satin stitches, using Black-Green chain stitch for veins and Black-Green tiny satin stitch in center of flowers. Outline darker ones with Emerald chain stitch, fill with Olive (1-strand) and Green (1-strand) satin stitches.

*This is the most complicated of all the designs; therefore, it might be wise to leave it to the last. The pattern would make a wonderful rug or quilt. [E.H.]

Ranunculus

Ranunculus

Color		Name	Type
1	Eggshell	Marlitt	Rayon
2	Blush Pink	Marlitt	Rayon
3	Pale Pink	Marlitt	Rayon
4	Medium Pink	Marlitt	Rayon
5	Pink	Persian	Wool
6	Dark Burgundy	Marlitt	Rayon
7	Dark Green	Marlitt	Rayon
8	Grass Green	Persian	Wool

STITCHES

Outline flower with Blush Pink chain stitch. Fill with slanted satin stitches of Dark Burgundy, Pale Pink, Medium Pink, Eggshell, and Pink Persian (2-strands). *Leaves*: Fill with Grass Green (2-strands) satin stitches, using Dark Green chain stitch for veins. Use Dark Green satin stitches for background of leaves.

Rosa „Rose”

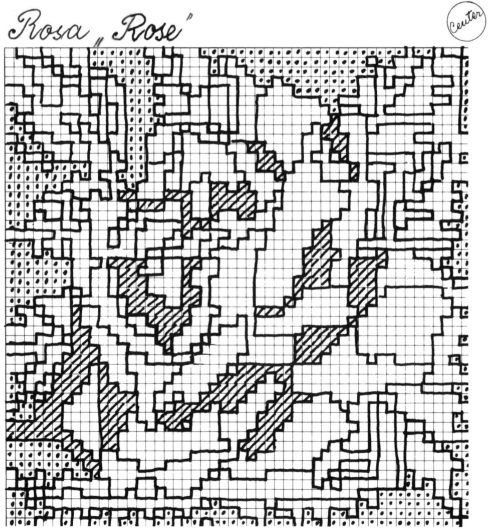

Rose

Rosa

	Color	Name	Type
1	Gold	Marlitt	Rayon
2	Light Yellow	Persian	Wool
3	Lemon	Persian	Wool
4	Gold	Persian	Wool
5	Orange	Mohair	Wool
6	Lime	Knitting	Acrylic
7	Light Green	DMC Floss	Cotton
8	Dark Green	DMC Floss	Cotton
9	Medium Green	Persian	Wool

STITCHES

Outline flowers and buds with Gold Marlitt chain stitch. Fill with slanted satin stitches of Light Yellow (white areas), double-strand Lemon (hatched areas), Gold Persian (light gray areas) and Orange in dark gray areas. *Leaves*: Use Lime chain stitch for outline and veins. Fill lighter leaves with Dark Green (doubled) satin stitches; fill darker leaves with Medium Green satin stitches. *Buds*: Yellows in buds are separated by Light Green slanted satin stitches. *Background*: Use Dark Green satin stitch.

Chrysanthemum maximum
„Shasta Daisy"

Center

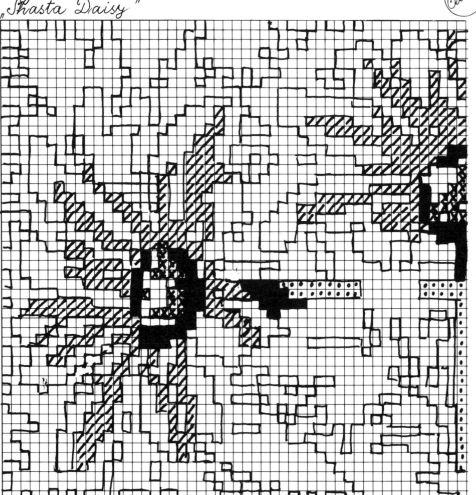

Shasta Daisy

Chrysanthemum maximum

	COLOR	NAME	TYPE
1	White	DMC Pearl #8	Cotton
2	White	Mohair	Wool
3	Light Gray	Persian	Wool
4	Lemon	Persian	Wool
5	Orange	Persian	Wool
6	Black	DMC Pearl #8	Cotton
7	Lime	Persian	Wool
8	Green	Persian	Wool
9	Emerald	Persian	Wool
10	Dark Green	Marlitt	Rayon

STITCHES

Outline flowers with White DMC chain stitch. Fill with White Mohair and Light Gray satin stitches. *Flower centers*: Use Lemon and Orange French knots, surrounded by Black satin stitches. *Leaves*: Outline with Dark Green chain stitch. Fill dark gray areas with Green satin stitches; fill black areas with Emerald satin stitches. *Stems* (hatched area): Lime satin stitches.

Helianthus „Sunflower"

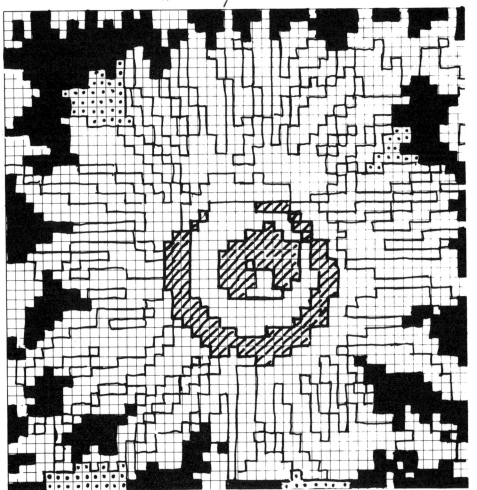

Sunflower

Helianthus

	Color	Name	Type
1	Yellow	Marlitt	Rayon
2	Lemon	Persian	Wool
3	Gold	Persian	Wool
4	Yellow Ochre	Persian	Wool
5	Light Green	Marlitt	Rayon
6	Dark Green	Persian	Wool
7	Blue	Marlitt	Rayon
8	Black	Marlitt	Rayon
9	Burgundy	Marlitt	Rayon
10	Red	Marlitt	Rayon

STITCHES

Outline flowers with Yellow chain stitch. Fill dark areas with Yellow slanted satin stitches; fill rest of flower with Lemon satin stitches. *Flower centers*: Use Dark Green satin stitches in the black areas, Light Green satin stitches in the hatched areas and Yellow Ochre (1-strand) satin stitches in the light gray area. On top of Dark Green make a circle of Yellow Marlitt French knots. *Background*: Put satin stitches of Blue and Black, threaded together, in cross-hatched area and Gold satin stitches in the hatched area. Use Burgundy (doubled) satin stitches in black area and Red satin stitches in light gray area.

Tulipa „Tulip"

Center

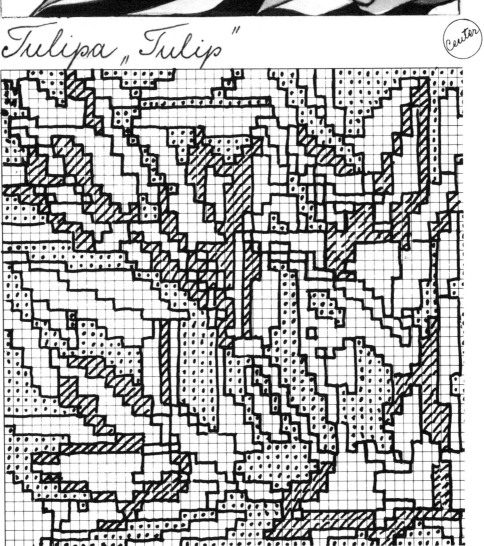

Tulip

Tulipa

	COLOR	NAME	TYPE
1	Yellow	Persian	Wool
2	Orange	Persian	Wool
3	Orange Red	Marlitt	Acrylic
4	Medium Red	Marlitt	Acrylic
5	Burgundy	Marlitt	Acrylic
6	Lime	Marlitt	Acrylic
7	Medium Green	Marlitt	Acrylic
8	Dark Green	Marlitt	Acrylic
9	Emerald	Marlitt	Acrylic
10	Black	Persian	Wool

STITCHES

Outline flowers in Yellow (1-strand) chain stitch. Fill-in with slanted satin stitches of Orange Red, Medium Red, and Burgundy. *Flower centers:* Yellow (hatched area) and Orange satin stitches, both 2-strand. *Leaves:* Outline with Lime chain stitch; fill with Medium Green, Dark Green, and Emerald satin stitches. *Background:* Black (2-strand) satin stitches.

69

Rosa Canina „Wild Rose"

center

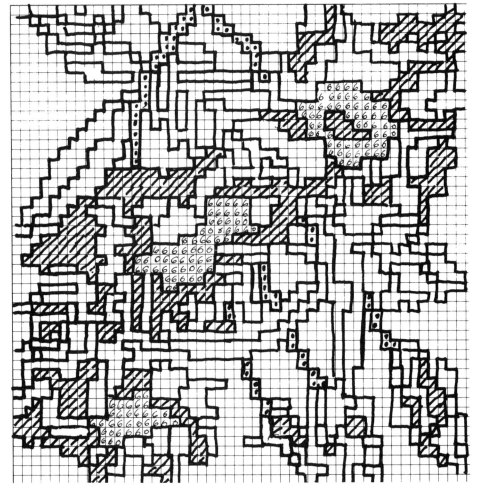

Wild Rose

Rosa Canina

	Color	Name	Type
1	Light Pink	Knitting	Acrylic
2	Medium Pink	Persian	Wool
3	Shocking Pink	Persian	Wool
4	Burgundy	Persian	Wool
5	Yellow	Persian	Wool
6	Orange	Persian	Wool
7	Light Green	Persian	Wool
8	Medium Green	Persian	Wool
9	Dark Green	Persian	Wool
10	Black	Persian	Wool

STITCHES

Outline all flowers with Shocking Pink (1-strand) chain stitch. Fill with the 3 shades of Pink in satin stitches. *Leaves* and *Veins*: Outline with Dark Green (1-strand) chain stitch. Fill with Light Green and Medium Green satin stitches. *Buds*: Outline with Dark Green (1-strand) chain stitch; fill with Light Green satin stitches at base of buds and Medium Pink satin stitches toward the tip. *Flower centers*: Yellow and Orange (1-strand) satin stitches. *Stems* and *Stamens*: Burgundy (1-strand) satin stitches.

Zinnia

center

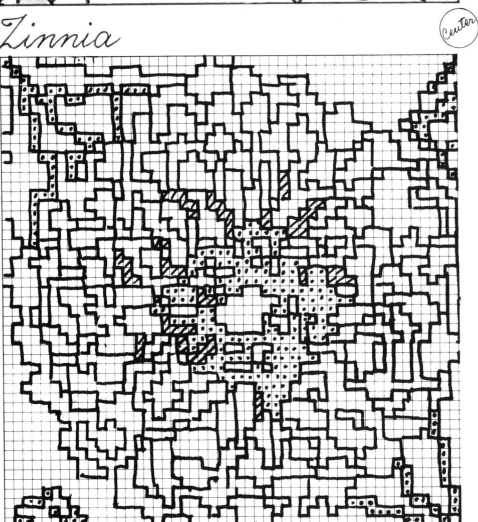

Zinnia

	COLOR	NAME	TYPE
1	Pink	DMC Pearl #8	Cotton
2	Yellow	DMC Pearl	Cotton
3	Medium Pink	Persian	Wool
4	Mexican Pink	Persian	Wool
5	Fuchsia	Persian	Wool
6	Magenta	Persian	Wool
7	Medium Burgundy	Persian	Wool
8	Dark Burgundy	Persian	Wool
9	Plum	Persian	Wool
10	Lime	Knitting	Acrylic
11	Medium Green	Persian	Wool
12	Olive	Persian	Wool
13	Grass Green	DMC Pearl #8	Cotton

STITCHES

Outline both lighter and darker flowers with Pink DMC chain stitch. Fill lighter flower petals with Medium Pink and Fuchsia satin stitches; fill darker flower petals with Mexican Pink and Magenta satin stitches—all colors in 2-strand. *Flower centers*: Use Dark Burgundy and Plum satin stitches, both 1-strand, and use Yellow in a combination of small satin stitches and French knots. *Hatched areas*: Use Lime satin stitch. *Leaves*: Outline with Grass Green chain stitch and fill with Olive satin stitches, using Medium Burgundy (1-strand) chain stitch for the veins. *Stems*: Outline with Grass Green (1-strand) chain stitch and fill with Medium Green satin stitches. *Buds*: Outline with Medium Burgundy (1-strand) chain stitch and fill with Medium Green (2-strand) satin stitches.

Iceland Poppy Circle.

Iceland Poppy Circle

NOTE: The folding technique used to reproduce and transfer to linen the thirty-two squares in the Flower-Bed Quilt, obviously does not apply to the nonsymmetrical Iceland Poppy Circle. Therefore, take the diagram of the latter to a photostat shop and have it blown up to a diameter of 22 inches. Then transfer a tissue-paper copy of the enlarged design to the center of a penciled square, 24½ inches by 24½ inches, which in turn has been centered on a 30-inch by 30-inch piece of Belgian linen. This is a large-scale design compared to the finer patterns of the thirty-two flower squares; consequently, it calls for larger needles, threaded with thicker yarns and used in bigger stitches with more over-stitching.

POPPY #1 (ORANGE)

	COLOR	NAME	TYPE
1	Yellow	Marlitt	Rayon
2	Yellow	Persian	Wool
3	Light Orange	Persian	Wool
4	Dark Orange	Persian	Wool
5	Lime	Persian	Wool
6	Dark Green	Persian	Wool
7	Hunter Green	Marlitt	Rayon
8	Dark Burgundy	Marlitt	Rayon

STITCHES

Outline flower with Yellow Marlitt chain stitch. Fill petals *first* with Dark Orange, next Light Orange, and then Yellow Persian satin stitches. All Persian yarns in these petals are doubled to 6-strands. *Flower center*: Use Lime satin stitches which radiate out from the center. Then use Dark Burgundy satin stitched in the same fashion. *Pistil*: Dark Green, Lime, and Hunter Green satin stitches. *Stamens*: Yellow Marlitt French knots.

POPPY #2 (PINK)

	COLOR	NAME	TYPE
1	Fuchsia	Marlitt	Rayon
2	Pink	Mohair	Wool
3	Mexican Pink	Persian	Wool
4	Fuchsia	Persian	Wool
5	Lime	Persian	Wool
6	Hunter Green	Marlitt	Rayon
7	Dark Burgundy	Marlitt	Rayon
8	Orange	Marlitt	Rayon

STITCHES

Outline flower with Fuchsia chain stitch. Using satin stitches, fill petals first with Fuchsia, second with Mexican Pink, and then Pink Mohair. All 3 yarns are doubled—the Persians to 6-strands, the Mohair to 2-strands. *Flower center*: Use Lime and Hunter Green satin stitches that radiate out from the center. *Stamens*: Dark Burgundy and Orange French knots.

POPPY #3 (ORANGE-RED)

	COLOR	NAME	TYPE
1	Orange	Marlitt	Rayon
2	Light Orange	Persian	Wool
3	Dark Orange	Persian	Wool
4	Orange-Red	Mohair	Wool
5	Lime	Persian	Wool
6	Dark Green	Persian	Wool
7	Hunter Green	Marlitt	Rayon
8	Dark Burgundy	Marlitt	Rayon

STITCHES

Outline flower with Orange chain stitch. Fill petals first with Orange-Red, second with Dark Orange, and then with Light Orange satin stitches. Double all Persian in petals to 6-strands and Mohair to 2-strands. *Flower center*: Use Lime and Hunter Green satin stitches that radiate out from the center. *Pistil*: Dark Green, Hunter Green, and Lime satin stitches. *Stamens*: Dark Burgundy and Orange French knots.

POPPY #4 (RED-BURGUNDY)

	COLOR	NAME	TYPE
1	Dark Burgundy	Marlitt	Rayon
2	Day-Glo Orange	Knitting	Acrylic
3	Orange-Red	Mohair	Wool
4	Dark Burgundy	Persian	Wool
5	Lime	Persian	Wool
6	Dark Green	Persian	Wool
7	Hunter Green	Marlitt	Rayon
8	Orange	Marlitt	Rayon

STITCHES

Outline flower with Dark Burgundy Marlitt chain stitch. Fill petals first with Dark Burgundy Persian (6-strands), second with Orange-Red Mohair (2-strands), and then with Day-Glo Orange (4-strands)— all in satin stitches. *Flower center*: Use Lime and Hunter Green satin stitches. *Pistil*: Dark Green and Lime satin stitches. *Stamens*: Orange French knots.

POPPY #5 (YELLOW)

	COLOR	NAME	TYPE
1	White	DMC Pearl #8	Cotton
2	Off-White	Mohair	Wool
3	Yellow	Persian	Wool
4	Gold	Persian	Wool
5	Lime	Persian	Wool
6	Dark Green	Persian	Wool
7	Orange	Marlitt	Rayon
8	Burgundy	Marlitt	Rayon

STITCHES

Outline flower with White chain stitch. Fill petals first with Gold (6-strands), second with Yellow (6-strands), and then with Off-White Mohair (2-strands)—all satin stitches. *Center of petals*: Lime and White satin stitches. *Flower center*: Use Lime satin stitch, with Dark Green chain stitches for the pistil. *Stamens*: Orange and Burgundy French knots.

POPPY #6 (YELLOW OCHRE)

	COLOR	NAME	TYPE
1	White	DMC Pearl #8	Cotton
2	Off-White	Mohair	Wool
3	Gold	Persian	Wool
4	Yellow Ochre	Persian	Wool
5	Lime	Persian	Wool
6	Olive	Marlitt	Rayon
7	Dark Burgundy	Marlitt	Rayon

STITCHES

Outline bud with White chain stitch. Fill petals first with Yellow Ochre (6-strands), second with Gold (6-strands), and then with Off-White Mohair (2-strands)—all in satin stitches. *Bottom of bud*: Fill with satin stitches of Dark Burgundy, Olive, Lime, White, and Off-White.

Center of Flower-Bed Quilt in Various Embroidery Stages

POPPY #7 (MAGENTA)

	COLOR	NAME	TYPE
1	Fuchsia	Marlitt	Rayon
2	Mexican Pink	Persian	Wool
3	Fuchsia	Persian	Wool
4	Plum	Persian	Wool
5	Lime	Persian	Wool
6	Dark Green	Persian	Wool
7	Hunter Green	Marlitt	Rayon
8	Orange	Marlitt	Rayon

STITCHES

Outline flower with Fuchsia Marlitt chain stitch. Fill petals first with Plum, second with Fuchsia Persian, and then with Mexican Pink—all 6-strand satin stitches. *Flower center*: Lime and Hunter Green satin stitches. *Stamens*: Orange French knots.

POPPY #8 (LIGHT PINK)

	COLOR	NAME	TYPE
1	White	DMC Pearl #8	Cotton
2	Blush Pink	Mohair	Wool
3	Light Pink	Persian	Wool
4	Mexican Pink	Persian	Wool
5	Dark Green	Persian	Wool
6	Lime	Persian	Wool
7	Dark Burgundy	Marlitt	Rayon
8	Orange	Marlitt	Rayon

STITCHES

Outline flower with White DMC chain stitch. Fill petals first with Mexican Pink (6-strands), second with Light Pink (6-strands), and then with Blush Pink Mohair (2-strands)—all satin stitches. *Flower center*: Lime satin stitches. *Pistil*: Lime and Dark Green satin stitches. *Stamens*: Dark Burgundy and Orange French knots.

Background: First fill-in veins with Lime chain (3 strands) stitches, then complete leaves with Black-Green (6 strands) satin stitches. You can substitute Mohair or even Angora for these Persian yarns should you desire more texture.

Chapter 4

Assembling the Flower-Bed Quilt

REQUIRED TOOLS

1. Quilting Needles, #8 or #9. Be sure they are short and sharp, with smooth, well-shaped eyes.

2. Straight Pins. Best quality steel with sharp points. Must be new to avoid possibility of rust stains.

3. Scissors. The sharper the better, for clean cutting is the secret to a well-made quilt. One large pair to cut fabric, a small pair for snipping loose threads and surplus ends of material.

4. Quilting Thread. I use only white because I like the added dimension of the light colored, running stitch.

5. Metal Thimble. Your finger is going to be in it for a long time, so pick a comfortable fit.

REQUIRED FABRICS

1. Five yards of 40-inch wide (or wider) textured, green cotton.

2. Five yards of grass-green cotton broadcloth, or linen if you prefer, for backing.

3. One king-size cotton flannel sheet for the quilt filling. If not available you may use cotton flannel yardage for the same purpose, but the widths will have to be pieced together.

INSTRUCTIONS

1. Cut six strips, 12 inches wide and 84½ inches long, from the green cotton.

2. One by one, take the six finished, needle-painted linen squares, on the far left of the quilt (consult Positioning Chart for exact order of flower squares) and, turning under the edge of each ½ inch, baste them onto the first 12-inch wide cotton strip–leaving 2½ inches between each square and at both ends of the strip.

3. Following the same procedure, baste flower squares to three more cotton strips to make the second row from the left, and rows one and two on the right-hand side of the quilt.

4. Once again, follow the same procedure for the two middle rows, only this time you must leave room for the Iceland Poppy Circle. Therefore, only four flower squares–two at the top and two at the bottom–are basted onto these 12-inch widths of cotton.

5. Cut seven 3-inch wide strips from the textured, green cotton material. These narrower pieces should also be 84½ inches long.

6. Now, take the two middle strips, turn under ½ inch on each side, and baste them to the 3-inch strips, ½ inch of which will overlap.

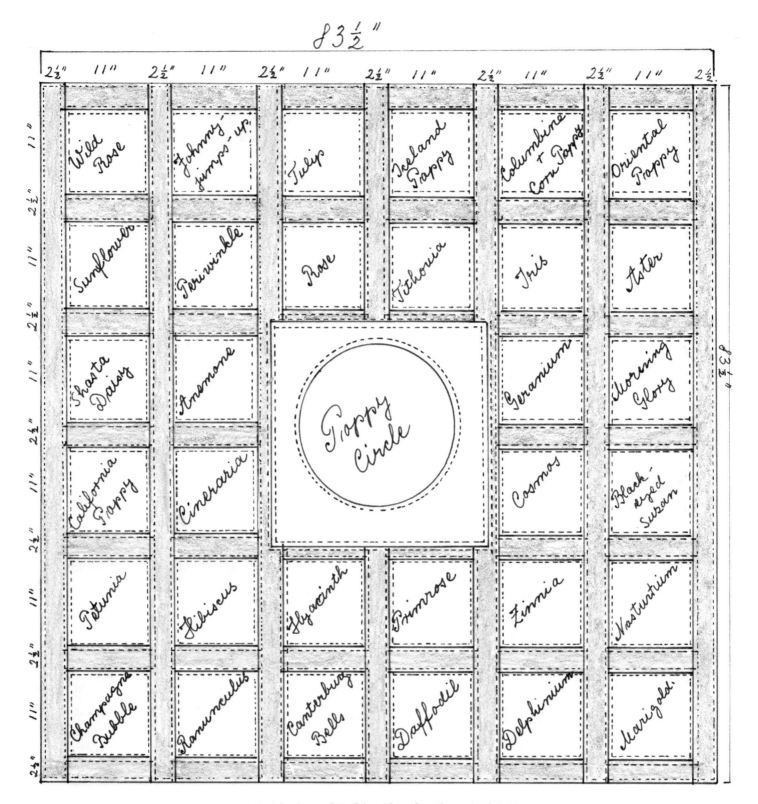

Positioning and Quilting Chart for Flower-Bed Quilt

7. Slip-stitch the eight flower squares on the two middle rows, which are now connected. Remove the basting stitches from the flower squares, a step which is repeated after each linen square is slip-stitched.

8. Take the 24½-inch Iceland Poppy Circle linen square and, after turning under ½ inch on all four edges, baste; then slip-stitch it in its proper position the exact center of the two center rows.

9. Attach the four remaining square-assembled rows—two on the left and two on the right of the middle two rows—to the 3-inch strips, following the same technique as in Step 6, above.

10. Slip-stitch the remaining twenty-four linen flower squares. The facing of the quilt is now completed.

11. Using a large, flat, smooth surface for a work table—a wooden floor is perfect for those who do not have the table—you are now ready to put together the three layers of the quilt.

12. Cut the grass green cotton broadcloth, or linen, if that is your choice, for the lining into two, 2½-yard lengths. Place them side by side and machine stitch together.

13. Place the king-size cotton sheet, the filler, on top of the lining. Put the quilt facing atop these two. Align the three layers of your double-decker quilt sandwich. Spread them smooth, pin them together, and baste the three with large stitches.

14. On the green textured cotton, surround every linen square—and the Poppy Circle square—with a row of white quilting stitches (also known as running stitch), 1/8th of an inch from the edge of the linen. (Use the dotted lines on the Positioning Chart as a guide to the placement of these and other quilting stitches.) Be sure your stitches go through all three layers of the quilt.

Running Stitch

15. Put in another row of quilting stitches, parallel to the ones in Step 14, 1/8th of an inch *inside* the edge of every linen flower square and the Poppy Circle square.

16. After removing all basting stitches, turn under the outside edges of the face of the quilt and the lining, ½ inch each. Snip off any excess filler, baste the top and lining together, and then slip-stitch together.

Flower-Bed Quilt As a Canopy or Shade

17. Finally, go around the entire perimeter of the quilt with a line of quilting stitches 1/8th of an inch from the edge.

NOTE: Some readers, having seen the instructions about the 12-inch and 3-inch wide cotton strips, may be wondering why they cannot simply piece together two widths of fabric and quilt-stitch the linen squares directly on that. They can, of course—just like you can machine stitch the entire quilt—but the finished product will be flatter and will have lost a good deal of its dimensional quality. I should also add that, although the quilt is washable, I have always played safe and had it dry cleaned.

Variation on the Flower-Bed Quilt

Chapter 5

Variations on the Flower-Bed Quilt

Should the multi-square Flower-Bed Quilt seem too grand an undertaking for starters, keep in mind that each of the floral patterns was designed to be used either in a quilt by itself (see the Marigold and Cineraria quilts), in multiples of itself (the Petunia quilt) or with a limited selection from among the thirty-two flower designs. Furthermore, you can also vary the texture of any given quilt by the use of plain appliqué or appliqué and trapunto (stuffing). For now, however, we will concentrate on making nine-square and five-square variations of the Flower-Bed Quilt.

In selecting the flower squares for inclusion in these modified quilts, try to choose according to the size of the design and/or the color of the flowers. The charts which follow were meant to help you in selecting compatible flower squares. How large you blow up the original designs depends, naturally, on the physical size of your intended quilt. Is it for a crib or a double bed? Also, to keep the design elements in proportion, the fewer the squares per quilt, the bigger the squares should be.

DESIGNS BY SIZE

LARGE	MEDIUM	SMALL
Oriental Poppy	California Poppy	Black-eyed Susan
Champagne Bubble	Shasta Daisy	Wild Rose
Iceland Poppy	Geranium	Morning Glory
Daffodil	Tithonia	Cosmos
Anemone	Marigold	Tulip
Sunflower	Champagne Bubble	Viola
Hyacinth	California Poppy	Nasturtium
Petunia	Vinca	Cineraria
Zinnia	Columbine and	Primrose
Rose	Corn Poppy	Delphinium
Iris	Hibiscus	
Ranunculus		

DESIGNS BY COLOR

YELLOW	YELLOW-ORANGE	RED
Shasta Daisy	Marigold	Geranium
Daffodil	Champagne Bubble	Hibiscus
Iceland Poppy	California Poppy	Tulip
Rose	Cosmos	Anemone
Sunflower	Nasturtium	Columbine and
Black-eyed Susan	Primrose	Corn Poppy
	Tithonia	

PINK-MAGENTA	MAGENTA to PURPLE	BLUES
Oriental Poppy	Canterbury Bells	Delphinium
Ranunculus	Aster	Morning Glory
Wild Rose	Viola	Iris
Zinnia	Petunia	Cineraria
		Hyacinth

WHITE ON WHITE

There are two white flowers in the Flower-Bed Quilt. However, if you like, as I do, to surround yourself with as much white as possible, any of the following flowers also come in white. So, you can switch their colors, as they appear in the thirty-two flowers, to various shades of white for a white-on-white quilt. In choosing yarns for such a project, you will find that the wools come in different degrees of off-white, while the acrylics come the closest to pure white. Also, the more textured your stitches with these yarns, the more gradations in "color" you will get in the white-on-white field.

Iceland Poppy	Geranium	Viola
Rose	Oriental Poppy	Petunia
Cosmos	Ranunculus	Iris
Primrose	Canterbury Bells	Delphinium
Tulip	Zinnia	Hyacinth
Anemone	Aster	Morning Glory
Hibiscus	Cineraria	

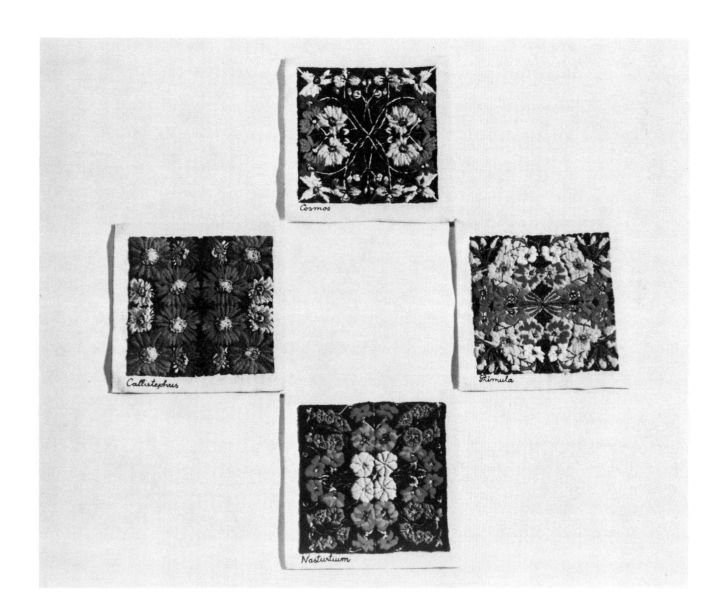

There is material enough in a single flower for the ornament of a score of cathedrals.   John Ruskin, 1851.

Nine Squares with the Large Flower Designs

The Nine-Square Quilt

In making this adaptation of the Flower-Bed Quilt, I selected my squares from the group of "large" flower designs. They are: Iris, Zinnia, Daffodil, Anemone, Iceland Poppy, Rose, Sunflower, Champagne Bubble, and Petunia. You can do this quilt in monochromes, using members of the same color family (shades of red, shades of yellow, etc.) or you can make it with a combination of whites, off-whites, shades of gray and beige and black. Or, you can stick with the multi-color approach of the Flower-Bed Quilt, itself.

The finished flower squares should be appliquéd on a darker background fabric, for instance, reds on burgundy or yellows on orange. I would use strips of a printed fabric, found in a yardage store, for the inside border, which is attached with quilting stitches. A favorite quotation or a dedication can be chain-stitched on the white, outside border. Choose a contrasting bright color for the lining.

The Five-Square Quilt

Here I decided upon squares from the "medium-size" flower designs: Tithonia, Marigold, Shasta Daisy, California Poppy, and Asters. Other than having fewer squares, the only difference between this quilt and the one above is that I suggest a white background and two prints, instead of one,

for the border, one of which also appears as a partial border to the floral squares, creating a three-dimensional effect. Again, you may pick a bright fabric for the lining or utilize one of the two prints from the border design.

Pillows and Cushions

Should you wish to start with something comparatively easy, before moving on to quilts and rugs, a flower-design pillow is an ideal warm-up exercise. They look wonderful on a plain white or neutral colored, large sofa. Putting one together is also quite simple.

1. Pick a colored fabric—cotton works well—which compliments the floral square you've embroidered.

2. Use the fabric to make a 16-inch by 16-inch pillow.

3. Fill it with kapok, Dacron, or down.

4. Line the flower square with sheer batiste before slip-stitching it onto the center of the pillow.

Now that is the washable version, for all you have to do is pull out the slip-stitch and remove the flower square before laundering the pillow case. If you do not mind sending it to the dry cleaners then the flower square can be permanently quilt-stitched or appliquéd to the pillow. However, in that case, the square is sewn to the background before you make and stuff the pillow.

Five Squares with the Medium Flower Designs

Anemone

Callistephus

Rudbeckia

California Poppy

Canterbury Bell.

Champagne Bubbles

Cineraria

Columbine with Poppy

Cosmos

Daffodil

Delphinium

Geranium

Hibiscus

Hyacinth

Papáver nudícaule

Iris

Viola

Tagetes erecta

Tithonia

Ipomoea

Nasturtium

Papáver orientále

Periwinkle

Petunia

Primula

Ranunculus

Rosa

Shasta Daisy

Helianthus

Tulipa

Rosa canina

Zinnia

Chapter 6

The Cineraria Quilt

The design of this one is the same as that found in the Cineraria pattern, except that it has two more flowers and, instead of a square shape, the elements fit the format of a king-size quilt, 6 feet 2 inches by 7 feet 4 inches, including the white border. You can make this same arrangement with any of the thirty-two floral designs in the portfolio.

I had the Cineraria square, one-quarter of it that is, blown up the easiest and quickest way possible—I took it to a blueprint shop. It is expensive, but you'll be saving a great deal of work and aggravation. You will still have to make a tracing of the blowup and for that you need heavy-duty tracing paper, the kind sold in art supply stores; a #2 pencil; and stick-pins to hold the tracing paper securely on top of the blowup. If you have a steady hand and are good at drawing, use a Pentel or Pilot fineline pen while tracing because you want a sharp, clearly defined impression. If not, go over the pencil tracing with a pen. Shade-in the different areas (see Cineraria, Chart 1) with hatching, cross-hatching, or black ink, which can be diluted to achieve shades of gray.

This quilt, and the Marigold one described in the following chapter, is strictly ornamental and the methods I followed in fabricating it are by no means the traditional ones. Just as with Needle-painting, I firmly believe it is the design which is the important element, not complicated techniques or sacred methodology. In short, it is fascinating to see an infinitely precise line of quilting stitches, but the joy is in the beauty of the total creative work.

The Cineraria Quilt was assembled on our dining-room table. I had previously decided upon the colors and selected the fabrics and now it was my turn to watch how a quilting expert, Sandy Fox, went about her craft. What follows is what I saw and what we did. In addition to the basic tools, listed at the beginning of chapter IV, you will need thumbtacks, several large sheets of carbon paper and light-weight cardboard, the kind laundries put in men's shirts. The list of required fabrics looked like this:

1. Two king-size white cotton percale sheets.

2. One king-size cotton flannel sheet or cotton flannel yardage, which will have to be pieced together.

3. One large bag of Dacron batting.

4. Two and one-half yards of Cornflower Blue cotton, enough to bind the quilt.

5. One and a half yards of the following cotton yardage (It might be wise to buy a little more of

2'6" (+7" wide border)

TOP CENTER.

3'2"   + 6" wide border

CENTER

#3
#6
#9
#2
#8
#5
#1
#4
#7

Detail of Cineraria Quilt

each to cover possible mistakes. Dye lots are hard to match, if you do run out of a particular color.): Royal Blue, Light Lavender, Dark Lavender, Purple, Turquoise, Bright Green, Olive Green, Emerald, and White (should be heavier than the rest, like a cotton duck).

6. One-half yard of cotton in each of the following colors: Black, Bright Yellow, Rust, and Light Blue.

NOTE: All the above materials must be color-fast and preshrunk or washed and dried with the machine set at HOT. Press *very* flat and smooth.

As you will see, every flower, leaf, and stem in this quilt is cut out separately and then appliqued in place. Since the all-over design calls for each floral element to be repeated four times, those who wish to avoid a quadruple load of tracing should make templates of the component parts (see cut-out patterns on Cineraria Charts II, III, and IV). To make a template, take the enlarged tracing of the floral element and, using carbon paper, make a copy of it on the cardboard. Then, using sharp scissors, cut out the cardboard template. With these at hand, you can begin cutting and assembling the quilt. A good deal of tacking down is required, so work on a surface which cannot be damaged. I use a large sheet of Celotex.

CUTTING AND STUFFING

1. Place template on well-ironed piece of fabric, reverse side up, and fasten in place with thumbtacks.

2. Carefully draw outline of template on fabric, using a well-sharpened piece of tailor's chalk or pencil.

3. Cut the fabric, leaving ¼ inch beyond the chalked line. Turn under this quarter-inch and baste. Snip off excess at corners.

4. Using a quilt stitch—basically a small running stitch, where the needle takes three or four stitches in a line before the thread is pulled through—sew one color fabric cut-out atop another, usually the lighter one on the darker. But, for the exact order of layering, consult the individual Leaf and Flower charts at the end of this chapter.

5. In cutting material for the elements which are to be stuffed (the flower centers and the areas where there is white fabric) leave ¾ inch, instead of ¼ inch, outside the template mark to allow room for generous stuffing.

6. Quilt-stitch the White fabric on top of the darker ones—Blue, Purple, Turquoise, and Laven-

der—leaving the edge, nearest the center of the flower, open.

7. Fill these white, finger-shaped pockets with Dacron batting, using a crochet needle to pack-in the stuffing. Then baste down the open edge. Whenever an edge does not show on the finished quilt surface, because another *quilt-stitched* fabric covers it, you may use basting stitches.

8. The centers of the flowers are stuffed as in Step 7, packing each layer—starting from the bottom—before adding and filling another.

9. The "dots" in the center of each flower were made by cutting tiny circles of fabric, filling them with minute pieces of batting, and tacking them in place with diminutive quilting stitches. I thought it would be much easier to fashion the "dots" from different size French knots but Sandy Fox, the purist, rejected my short-cut suggestion.

10. The stuffed centers of the flowers are now quilted on top of the white, stuffed petals, which, in turn, are quilted atop the darker (non-stuffed) outer edges of the flowers.

Now that the individual flowers have been constructed, it is time to put the quilt together.

ASSEMBLING THE QUILT

1. Find the exact center of the top of the quilt—one of the cotton percale sheets, the other is used as backing—by folding the sheet exactly in half, first horizontally and then vertically. Run a large basting stitch along the crease marks. These two guidelines are needed to help you layout exactly the component parts of the Cineraria design.

2. When placing the design elements and when doing the actual quilting, start from the center and work out toward the perimeters. I did mine freehand, using a yardstick to be sure the design compositions, in all four quarters of the quilt, were of an equal distance from the intersecting guidelines of basting stitches. Anything handmade has certain inaccuracies, which is part of its charm, so do not be concerned if you are off an eighth of an inch here and there.

3. The precut leaves and stems, with their ¼ inch tucked under and their edges basted, are positioned first. Keep them in place with straight pins and then large basting stitches. Once firmly set, sew them on with small quilting stitches.

4. Again, using pins and basting stitches, position and tack down the individual flowers atop their background of leaves and stems. Permanently attach them with a single line of small quilting

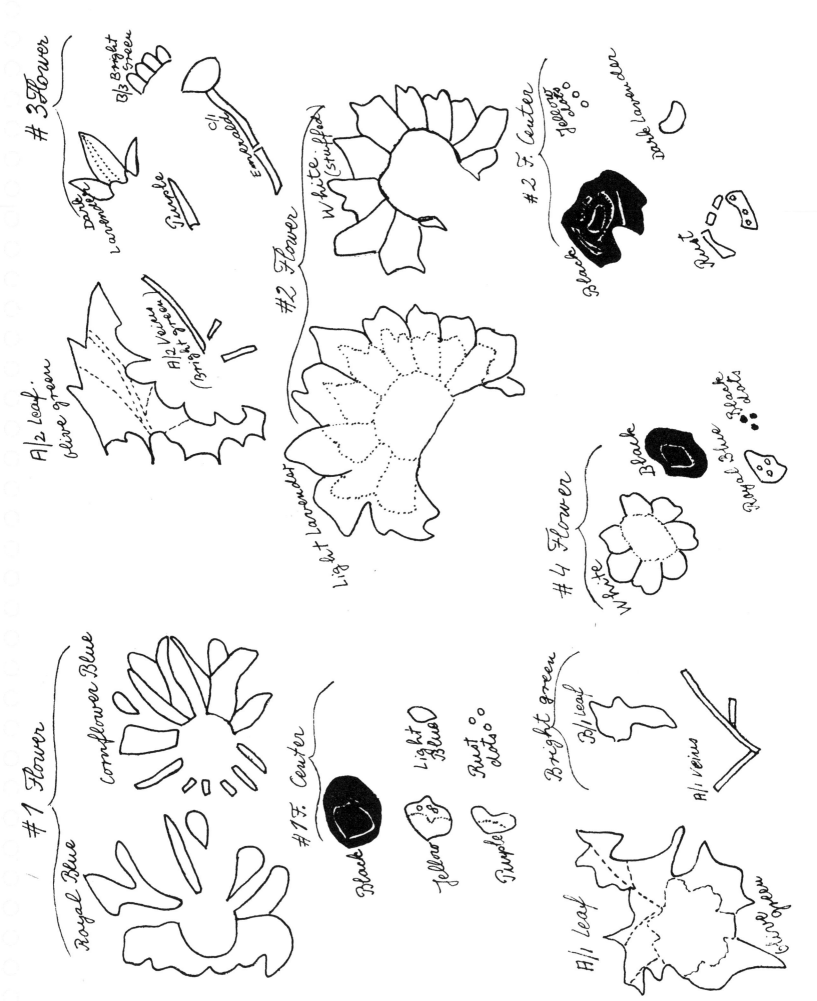

3 Flower

B/3 Bright Green

Dark Lavender

Purple

C/1 Emerald

#2 Flower

White (stuffed)

A/2 Leaf Olive green

A/2 Veins (Bright green)

Light Lavender

#2 F. Center

Yellow dots

Dark Lavender

Black

Rust

#4 Flower

Black

Royal Blue Black dots

White

#1 Flower

Cornflower Blue

Royal Blue

#1 F. Center

Black

Light Blue

Yellow

Rust dots

Purple

Bright green

B/1 Leaf

A/1 veins

A/1 Leaf

Green

Templates for the Nine Flowers in the Cineraria Quilt

#6 Flower

Center

Black

Royal Blue

Yellow

Black

Light Blue

Black dots

Turquoise

#5 Flower

Center: Royal Blue

Yellow

Light Blue °° Dots

White (stuffed)

Dark Lavender

c/2 veins Bright Green

c/2 Leaf

Emerald

#7 (Center) Flower

Center:

Emerald

4 Green dots

Yellow

Light Blue dots

Emerald

Purple

White (stuffed)

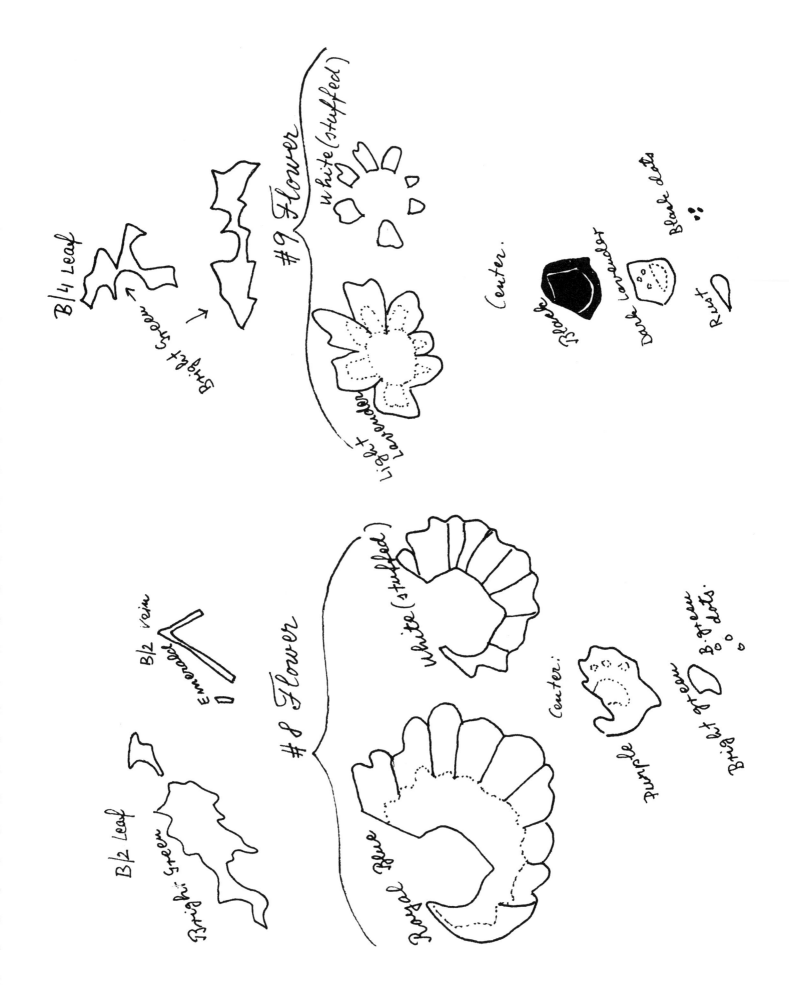

B/4 Leaf

Bright green

#9 Flower

white (stuffed)

Light Lavender

Center.

Black

Dark Lavender

Black dots

Root

B/2 vein

B/2 Leaf

Bright green

Emerald

#8 Flower

white (stuffed)

Royal Blue

Center.

Purple

Bright green

B. green dots.

95

stitches. The first flower to tack down is, of course, the center one, #7 on the Cineraria Charts. The top of the quilt is now finished and must be attached to its other layers.

5. Find a large flat area—the floor again—and stretch out the king-size percale sheet which is to serve as the backing. The flannel sheet is placed on top of that and, finally, the quilt top, face up. Both backing and filler should extend beyond the edges of the quilt top.

6. Smooth out all three layers, as evenly as possible, then pin and baste them together. A row of basting stitches around the perimeter, one vertical and one horizontal row through the quilt center and two diagonal lines of basting stitches, are required to keep the layers firmly in place.

7. Quilt two rows, on the white sheeting, around the entire design. The first row should be 1/8 inch from the edge of the design; the second, 1/4 inch from the first row. Be sure your stitches go through all three layers of the quilt sandwich.

8. Remove all basting stitches and trim off any of the cotton filler which protrudes beyond the edges.

9. Then, to edge the quilt, cut four 1½-inch wide strips from the Cornflower Blue cotton. Two of them should be 7 feet 4 inches long, two of them should be 6 feet 6 inches long.

10. Miter the ends of the strips where they join at the four corners of the quilt. Fold under ¼ inch of the blue strips, on both sides, and wrap around the quilt edge, sewing it to the top *and* bottom sides with small quilting stitches. Of course, if you prefer, instead of cutting your own edging material, you can use ready-made blanket binding, woven binding, or bias edging.

NOTE: There are other places to use quilts than on top of a bed. I have hung the Cineraria Quilt on the wall *behind* our bed. It stays flat and in shape because brass curtain rods were inserted in sleeves, sewn to the back of the quilt, top and bottom.

ORDER TO FOLLOW IN QUILTING LEAVES AND STEMS (Refer to Charts)

1. A/1 and A/2: Dark Olive Green
2. B/1: Bright Green
3. B/4: Bright Green
4. B/2: Bright Green (Leave lower part open to slip over edge of flower #8.)
5. C/2: Emerald
6. C/1: Emerald (goes on top of A/2)

ORDER TO FOLLOW IN QUILTING FLOWERS (Refer to Diagrams)

Flower 1: Royal Blue on top of Cornflower Blue. Center: Light Blue on Purple, Purple on Yellow, Yellow on Black. Rust dots on Yellow.

Flower 2: White on Light Lavender. Center: Dark Lavender on Black and Rust on Black. Yellow dots on Rust.

Flower 3: A bud. Purple on Dark Lavender, Bright Green (stuffed) on Dark Lavender and Purple. Emerald on Bright Green.

Flower 4: White petals. Center: Royal Blue on Black. Black dots on Royal Blue.

Flower 5: White on Dark Lavender. Center: Light Blue on Royal Blue. Yellow dots on Royal Blue.

Flower 6: Turquoise on Royal Blue. Center: Light Blue on Black, Black on Yellow, Yellow on Black. Black dots on Light Blue and Yellow.

Flower 7: White on Purple. Center: Emerald on Yellow. Yellow on Emerald. Light Blue dots on Emerald and Bright Green dots on Yellow.

Flower 8: White on Royal Blue. Center: Bright Green on Purple. Bright Green dots on Purple.

Flower 9: White on Light Lavender. Center: Rust on Dark Lavender, Dark Lavender on Black. Black dots on Dark Lavender.

Chapter 7

The Marigold Quilt

Here is another needlework project which grew out of the Flower-Bed Quilt. In this case, I modified the yellow and orange marigold square, lifting the bud in the top center of the original design three inches to fit a vertical format. Also, the original drawing of the marigolds looked so good in black and white that I was encouraged to make a quilt without color. Actually, any of the floral designs in the portfolio can be executed in this fashion. It would be quite beautiful to needlepaint a quilt, let's say with just eight squares, following this approach. Naturally, working with only two colors simplifies your task tremendously.

The finished size of this quilt is 6 feet 1 inch by 6 feet 4 inches, with the design itself measuring 3 feet 4½ inches by 3 feet 8½ inches. It fits both king- and queen-size beds. To give this two-color quilt another dimension, I used a natural, un-bleached muslin for the background material. The subtle difference is just enough to set off the white.

The process of tracing and enlarging the design is much the same as that followed in the Cineraria Quilt. However, here the design was flip-flopped four times and, with the aid of dressmaker carbon paper, traced directly on the muslin. Then I went over the markings with a Pilot fineline pen. Those who are used to working with an iron-on transfer pen may prefer to do it that way. Because so much of this quilt is embroidered, a freehand copying of the design on the muslin will not work. For the same reason, plus the fact that you are using only two colors, layering charts are not needed. Do remember, though, to make accurate templates, once the design is enlarged to the desired size.

MATERIALS NEEDED

2¼ yards of unbleached muslin (I used the 78-inch width, but it comes even wider.)
1½ yards of White cotton broadcloth
1½ yards of Black cotton broadcloth
2½ yards of Black and White patterned cotton
2½ yards of Black and White border design cotton
4½ yards of Black on White polka dot cotton, for lining
8½ yards of Black cotton cording
1 king-size flannel sheet or cotton flannel by the yard
Black DMC Embroidery Floss
Black DMC #8 Pearl Cotton
White quilting thread
NOTE: All materials on the above list should be preshrunk and well ironed before use.

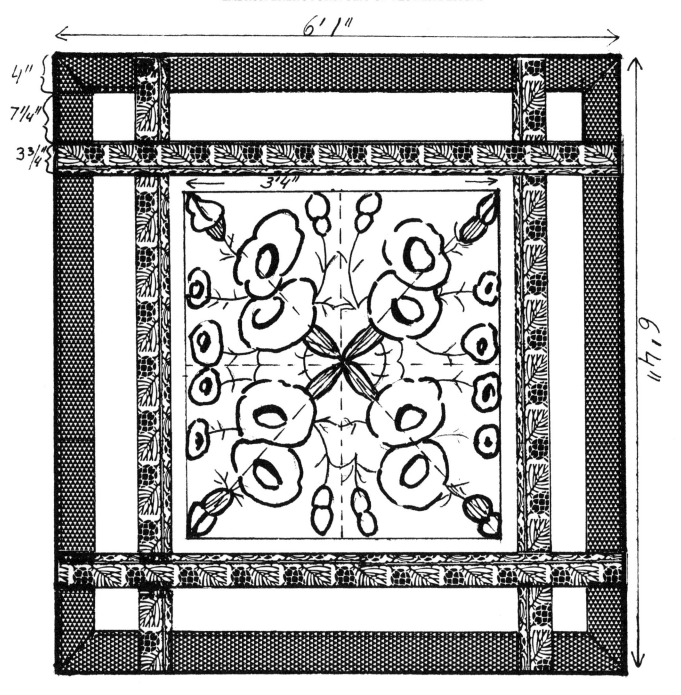

Positioning Chart for the Marigold Quilt

SCALE: 1"=1'.

Once again, how well you cut out the petals is very important. Be sure your edges are sharp and clean and that ¼ inch is left beyond the cutting line, so that the fabric can be tucked under. None of the petals or flowers are stuffed in this quilt, therefore the ¼-inch overage is constant throughout. Because the petals are so small, and the fabric is the same on both sides, you can cut a stack of them at the same time. Start with four to test your multiple-cutting prowess.

TOP CENTER

3'

3'6"

CENTER

Diagram for the Marigold Quilt

Detail of Marigold Quilt

The appliquéing can be done two ways. Petal by petal, or by cutting the whole flower out of the Black broadcloth, using the template and white tailor's chalk to mark where the White petals go, and quilting the latter in their proper places. The petal by petal method is more work, but the textured, dimensional effect you end up with is well worth the effort. Start at the outside edge of each flower and go around the perimeter, quilting down the Black petals. Then, move in a bit and go around again, affixing the White petals on top of the Black ones. Continue this circular course and you will eventually quilt-on the last fabric cut-out in the center of the flower. When the White petals overlap other White petals, they are outlined with a stem stitch, using two-strand, Black cotton floss.

The leaves, stems, and stamens are embroidered onto the cotton duck: the stamens, with Pearl Cotton #8, Black; and the leaves and stems with six-strand, Black cotton floss—couched with a single strand. Chain stitches would be just as effective, providing they are small, even, and fluid. They cer-

tainly are a lot easier than couching. With the floral elements of the quilt completed, you now cut the strips, turn under ¼ inch of the fabric, and slip-stitch them in place on the muslin. Naturally, if a small quilt is desired, omit the strips and, conversely, if you are working on a bigger quilt than this one, strips may be added.

To finish this quilt, cut the polka dot lining into two, 2¼-yard lengths and piece together. Lay this on a flat surface, put the flannel sheet over it, and top with the completed cotton-duck layer. Align the three layers, smooth them flat, and crisscross them with basting stitches so that they hold their position. The design—both the appliquéd and the embroidered elements—must now be outlined with a row of quilting stitches. Use White thread and go through the three tiers of the quilt. This row of quilting stitches should be 1/8th of an inch beyond the end of the marigold design.

Finally, after pulling out the basting stitches and trimming any protruding pieces of filler, turn under ½ inch of the outside edges of the top and bottom layers of the quilt and insert, between them, the Black cotton cording. Slip-stitch both edges to the cording and finish with a row of quilting stitches, 1/8th inch from the cord.

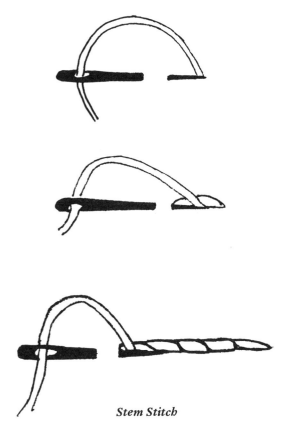

Stem Stitch

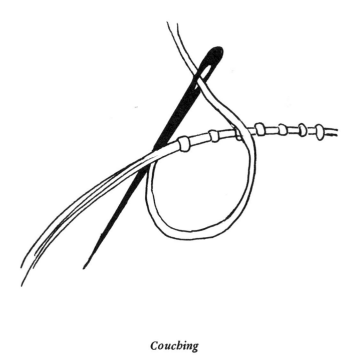

Couching

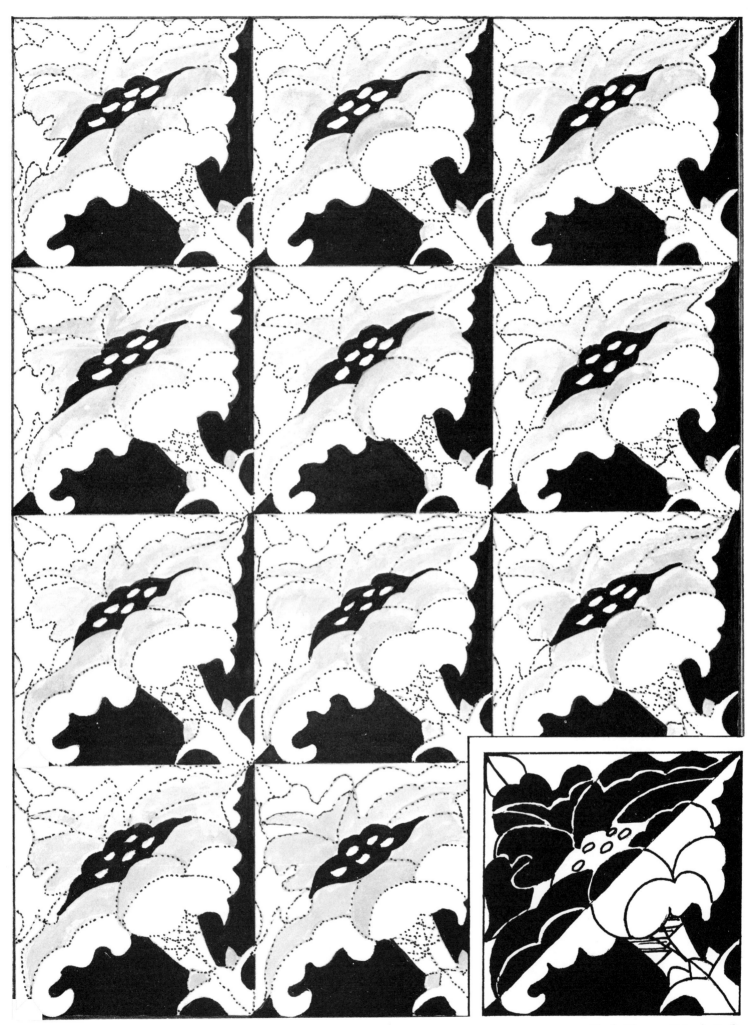

Single Blossom Petunia Quilt

Chapter 8

Quilts in the Works

The quilt possibilities, stemming from those original flower squares, seem to go on forever. I am particularly intrigued with what happens when you play with just a single, isolated element in the floral designs. It is a game that everyone interested in the needlecrafts can enjoy, for the stakes are low (a few dollars worth of materials and working at something you like) and you get to keep the winnings—for years and years to come.

At the present time, I am participating in four of these games, with newly designed, single-element quilts in different stages of production. This brief chapter is devoted to drawings of each, along with an explanation of how I visualize the quilts in their finished form. At the rate I am taking to write this book, I would not be surprised—but I would be delighted—if some readers complete quilts based on these suggestions long before I do. But the challenge is not limited to quilt makers. All of the ideas can be translated into gros point or hooked rugs, or a combination of both.

The Petunia Quilt

You will notice that this one (facing page) is a repeat design of a single blossom found in the Petunia square. I find the multiple rendering very dramatic, graphically, but I also realize that it would not go in every room. If that's the case, you might wish to quilt just one giant petunia (see below), a classic Art Nouveau handling.

I can imagine these two versions done only in black and whites: black polished cotton, white chintz with stuffing (the white areas), and white duck (gray areas)—the entire design to be stitched with white. Or, for those who want something very luxurious, I would use black velveteen, white satin, white linen and I would edge the quilt with a brilliant green velveteen.

104

The Hyacinth Quilt

Here again (see opposite page) I have blown up and slightly modified part of a flower design. Make the quilt in much the same fashion as the marigold one was executed; instead of having a white sheet for the top layer, however, use a fine print fabric for the flower petals and the quilt surface. The leaves and flower centers should be cut from a plain fabric. The prints used can be black and white or colored, since hyacinths actually come in light and dark blue, lavender, purple, white, cream, pink, magenta—you name it. Whichever color combination you settle upon, the black areas on the drawing—between the flower petals—should be a dark shade of the print color; for example, pink petals require magenta shadows. The centers should be the same color as the shadows, but outline them with black couching. For the leaves, use three different shades of green: bright, emerald, and dark. I would border the quilt with the same dark color used for the petal shadows or with any of the greens. All the fabrics used in the Hyacinth Quilt should be cotton.

106

The Canterbury Bells Quilt

This should be the easiest to make of all the quilts. Two different prints were used, one for the flower background, the other for the stamen and scalloped quilt border. The blossom and its stamen elements are stuffed according to the method followed in the Cineraria Quilt. Live Canterbury Bells are blue, purple, pink, or white; however, you can forget botanical accuracy and make them any color you like. Let us say you decide on purple, then use a light shade of purple for the white portion (see opposite page) of the petals, a medium purple in the gray areas. The black lines on the flower face should be couched with a very dark purple, wool yarn. Although, if you plan to wash the quilt, switch to cotton couching. Medium green would be right for the leaves and dark green for the stem and sepal leaves. I would use a vivid, grass green print for the stamens and the scalloped border. For the edging, use a fabric which matches the color of the couching yarn.

The Zinnia Quilt

A single round flower makes a singular round quilt. Other blossoms from the Flower-Bed Quilt which lend themselves to a circular format are: Ranunculus, Anemone, Sunflower, and the Oriental Poppy. I used (see page opposite) five different fabrics in the composition of the Zinnia—three were differing small prints and two were plain. Zinnias come in every color of the rainbow, even green, so pick your fancy. Be sure, however, that both the prints and the plains are shades of the same color. The white areas on the drawing are stuffed as well as the black part of the center. The whole quilt should have the feeling of a giant, puffed up cushion.

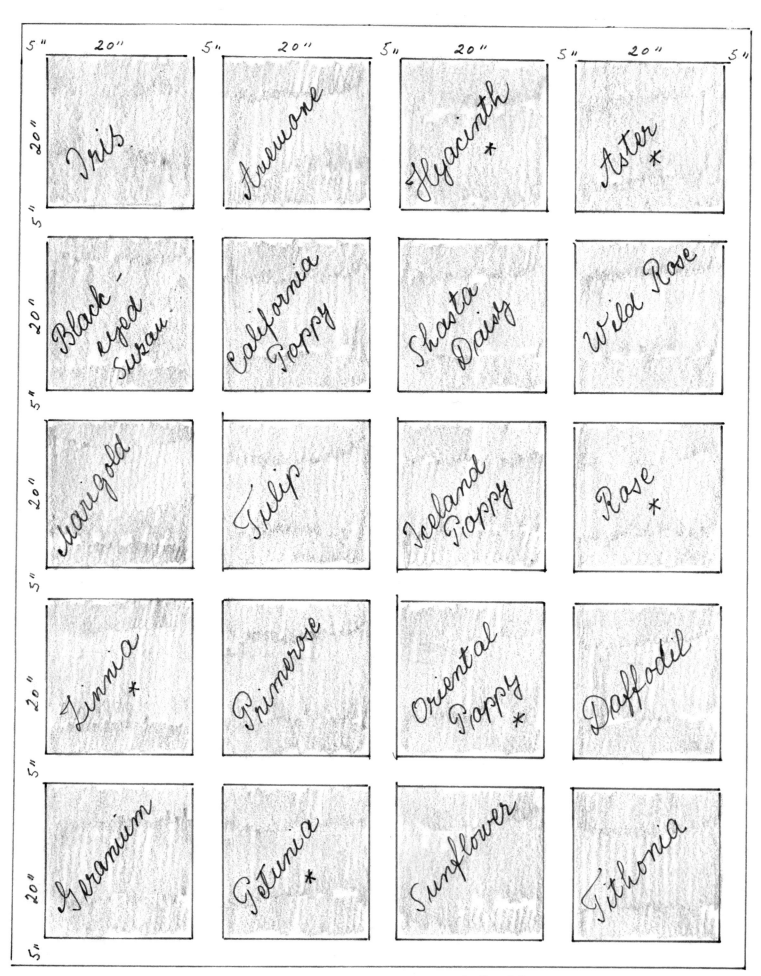

Position Chart for the Flower Bed Rug, 10'10" X 8'9"

Chapter 9

Rugs: Gros Point, Embroidered, and Hooked

I must assume, for the sake of textual brevity, that any reader wanting to undertake a rug project, based on the designs in this book, has had some experiences in the basics of the craft. To do otherwise, to write a complete primer on the art of rug making, would tax the binding of this volume.

Therefore, in this chapter, I shall be providing a *general* how-to account of what went on in the making of the Flower-Bed Rug and the Poppy Circle Rug. Craftsmen, who have one rug under their belts, or feet in this case, should have no difficulty in following through on their own.

Flower-Bed Rug

It measures 10 feet 10 inches by 8 feet 9 inches and is composed of twenty squares from the original thirty-two Flower-Bed Quilt designs. (See Positioning Chart for exactly which ones.)

MATERIALS

Canvas: Double, also called Penelope. Fifteen yards, 40 inches wide with five holes to the inch.
Yarns: Paternaya Persian Rug Yarn, Gigantic Wool Rug Yarn, and Multi-Craft Acrylic Rug Yarn. (Yarn shop salespeople are very good at estimating how much you will need for a particular project.)

Hooking Wool: White, 2-inch precut for hooking. You'll need approximately five packages per square foot of hooked area.
Miscellaneous: Upholstery cotton, approximately seven yards. Binding, forty feet, 2 inches wide. Felt and lining (optional).

Again, as in needlepainting, the yarns were chosen primarily for their colors. If I could not find a particular shade in the rug yarns then I switched to regular Persian and/or knitting yarns and squeezed into the needle eye as many strands of the latter as possible. For example, I threaded my needle with 9-ply Persian embroidery yarn and with 2-ply

Acrylic Rug Yarn. However, the background for all the squares should be flat, so I used 1-ply Gigantic Wool Rug Yarn in very dark green for those areas. Latch hooking was used for the centers in the following flowers: Zinnia, Cosmos, Iceland Poppy, Shasta Daisy, Oriental Poppy, Sunflower, Anemone, Black-eyed Susan, and Tithonia.

I wanted a rug with warm colors and whites; consequently, I avoided blue flowers or changed their color from the original squares. This was done with the following:

Hyacinth: From blues and lavenders to whites and pinks.

Aster: From blues and purples to yellows, oranges, and rust tones.

Rose: From yellow to red.

Zinnia: From pinks and magenta to yellows and greens.

Petunia: From deep purples to whites and grays.

Oriental Poppy: From light pinks to shocking pinks and reds.

With the exception of the above, the colors remained the same as those in the needlepainted squares, or as close as you can get to them with rug yarns. It goes without saying that there is nothing mandatory about the above color combinations. Should you desire a rug for a cool, blue room, simply reverse what I did and accent the blues, purples, and lavenders. Or you can do the rug in all whites or all yellows.

Each rug square is 20 inches by 20 inches, exactly double the size of those in the quilt. Depending upon what sort of project you want the squares for—and how much time you are willing to expend—their size can be changed simply by switching the type of canvas you work with. If you use the 10/20 Penelope or the #10 mono instead of the 5 to 1, you get one-half the size of the rug squares, or a 10-inch by 10-inch segment. Naturally, the larger the holes the quicker it goes. On the other hand, if you want marvelous little pillows, the finer the weave the better.

The fifteen yards of canvas were cut into five, three-yard pieces, and the edges were taped to avoid unravelling. Each three-yard strip contains four squares (see color photograph with five strips). Those who helped me needlepoint the squares worked from charts and counted the repeats. All four repeats are identical. Then again, you can paint the design on the canvas with acrylics, if you are not a stickler for precision.

Because texture for me is just as essential to good design as color, after the squares were needle-pointed, I over-embroidered each of them. For veins and stems, use chain stitches on top of the needlepoint; for flowers, large satin stitches. The stamens get large French knots. There is no hard and fast rule about this added embellishment. Simply pick one dominant color—or two— from the design and over-embroider, but don't overdo it. After all, you want the needlepoint to show through as well. If you do not like the idea of

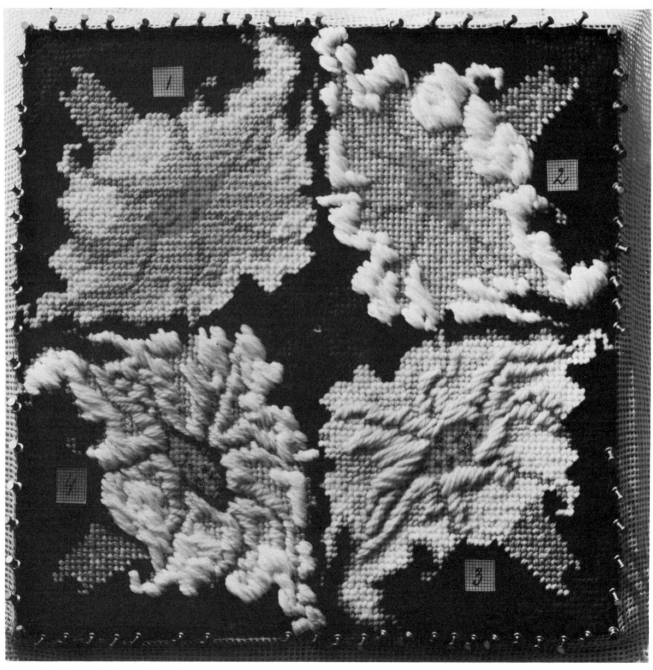

Over-embroidery of a Gros-Point Square

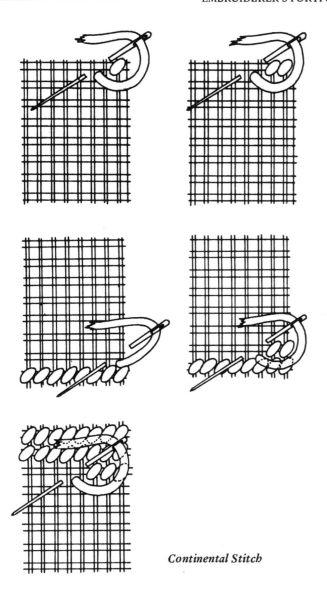

Continental Stitch

bottom, and 5 inches of empty canvas on either side. When putting the five strips together, overlap the empty 5-inch sides 2½ inches each, align the canvas holes carefully, and with large machine stitches sew them together. This keeps them in place for easy hooking. Next, using the white pre-cut wool, latch-hook all of the "in-between" 5-inch areas of the rug. However, before you latch-hook the outer edges of the rug with white wool, turn under 3 inches of the empty canvas—once again aligning the holes carefully. In this way you achieve a neat, firm edge.

I lined the Flower-Bed Rug myself, and my advice to you is that if you can afford it, have that final step done by an upholsterer. If not, suffer along with me. First I sewed 2-inch cotton seam binding all around the bottom edge. Then, after covering the bottom surface with a layer of cotton felt, I covered that with a cotton print lining and hand-stitched both to the seam binding. Finally, from the corners of each square on the face of the rug, I pulled through to the back a heavy strand of dark green Persian and tied it with three or four knots, thus keeping the three layers of the rug firmly in place.

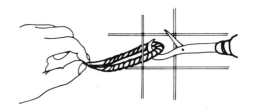

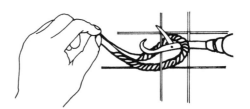

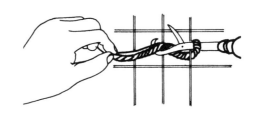

Latch Hook

over-embroidery, yet still desire more texture, you can hook in other areas beside the center or hook the entire rug, for that matter. It all depends what you are best at and which surface satisfies you aesthetically.

After all the needlework was completed on the squares, they were blocked like the ones for the needlepainted quilt, only instead of washing them I used a damp sponge on the back side and a staple gun rather than push pins, to block. After the canvas was dry, a steam iron was held over, not on, the squares to fluff up the yarn.

ASSEMBLING THE RUG

On each of the five strips, made up of four gros point squares (see color illustration at front of book), leave 8 inches of empty canvas, top and

Poppy Rug As a Wall Hanging

The Poppy Circle Rug

MATERIALS

Canvas: Four and one-half yards of #4 (four holes to the inch) Quick Point canvas, 40-inch or 42-inch width.

Yarns: Gigantic Wool Rug Yarn and Multi-Craft acrylic Rug Yarn. Dark green, 2-inch precut wool for background; Light green, 2-inch precut for veins in background (approximately five packages per square foot).

Miscellaneous: Latch hook; 2½ yards of bias seam binding, 2 inches wide; liquid Latex (one quart covers nine square feet); a 7-inch and a 3-inch to 4-inch scissors.

Six feet in diameter, this rug is a blown-up version of the circle-in-the-square, found in the middle of the Flower-Bed Quilt (see color illustration at front of book), adapted for latch hooking. Of course, it can be done with gros point, if a flat rug is preferred. But this treatment is far more lush and the colors are more brilliant because, when the pile is cut, all the yarns are exposed to light. The colors used are the same, or as near as possible, to those in the needlepainted circle.

Try to find as many colors as you can in wool, since it is soft, durable, and springs back. Acrylics, on the other hand, are more economical, and the colors are brighter, more shimmering, and never fade. So, if the rug is to be used for heavy-duty areas, buy wool; if it is being done as a wall hanging, acrylic is the answer. Mine is a mixture of both yarns. When you find a yarn you like, consider buying it by the box. It is cheaper that way, you eliminate the chance of not being able to locate the exact color again, and what you do not use up in the rug can be saved for a future project. Before calling in my gang of hookers—if you'll pardon the expression—I did the following:

1. After the design was enlarged by the photostater to a circle six feet in diameter, I colored-in the print with acrylic paints.

2. I cut the 4½ yards of canvas in half and pieced the two lengths together with large machine stitches, being careful that the holes were in alignment, and then taped all four edges with masking tape.

3. I placed the canvas down on the floor, on top of the painted photostat. To hold both steady and in place, I put tailor's weights (weighty books will do) along the edge of the canvas.

4. Using acrylic paint, I copied the pattern on to the canvas.

The background of the circle design was hooked with the precut dark green and light green yarns. The pile in that area is ¾ inches high. However, the rest of the yarns had to be cut by hand, because I wanted a high pile, carved finish. Having determined how high a pile you want, double that figure and add ½ inch for the knot. In other words, I cut 8½-inch lengths because I wanted to end up with a 4-inch pile, before carving. To simplify this massive cutting operation, wind the yarn around a heavy piece of cardboard which is *one half* the size of the desired length. Cut the carded loops once and you end up with a group of yarns all the correct length. I used rubber bands to collect mine in bundles of one hundred.

When the hookers had finished their labors, the end result looked like a giant, shaggy Old English sheep dog—in Technicolor. Before trying to make sense of this bewildering mess, I turned the rug over and applied a coating of Latex to the back, using a 2-inch painter's brush. Latch-hooked rugs really do not need a Latex under coat, but I wanted to be sure the knots were firmly enough in place to survive the strenuous carving sessions which lay ahead. Also, we have highly polished wood floors and Latex made the rug skid-proof.

Carving

116

Detail of Carving on Poppy Rug

117

Carving Guide for Poppy Rug

CARVING

I strongly suggest that you practice carving on a simple design before undertaking the Poppy Circle Rug, something like the white flowers against a blue background, black and white pictures of which appear on pages 116 and 117. I've also drawn a Carving Guide (see opposite page) to explain the process and indicate the lowest pile areas (the dotted sections of the drawing). I always begin carving on the perimeter of the flower because 1. The pile is always low at the edges, and 2. I establish immediately the dividing line between the flowers. Then I go directly to the centers.

In the Poppy Rug, the center surrounding the seed pod has the lowest pile level, the same ¾-inch height as the background. You could save yourself some work by finding the right colors in precut 2-inch yarn for this section. The seed pods are cut higher, about a 2-inch pile, and gently curved toward the surrounding center area. Then attack the petals, one by one (see detail of rug, color photograph). The darkest shade in the petal is always cut lower than the preceding lighter shade and the lightest shade is always the highest. The dark areas indicate a 1½-inch pile; the medium shaded areas, a 2½-inch pile, and the light sections, a 3½-inch pile. Those are the approximate finished heights, but in the first cutting leave them a little longer to give yourself leeway to perfect the carving.

The first cutting should be straight, parallel to the surface of the rug, and you need not measure the length with a ruler—unevenness is an asset. With the second cut, start shaping and curving the pile. This is the time-consuming part. Pause now and then to ruffle up the yarns with your hand, bringing the uneven strands into focus. The finished petals should have a rounded, velvety feeling, which comes with practice. With all the snipping that takes place, you seem to be wasting a great deal of yarn, but I know of no other way. I save the clippings and stuff pillows with them. It took me a good week to complete carving the Poppy Rug, because your hands cannot take more than two or three hours of this kind of exercise. As it was, after the first day my scissors-holding fingers were swathed in Band-Aids.

Once the rug was completely carved, I very carefully removed the masking tape, cut off any canvas in excess of 1½ inches, turned the unfinished edge under, and with large stitches and a heavy-duty yarn, sewed it to the bottom, hooked surface. Then, using the bias tape, I hemmed the whole, circular perimeter.